Wildfowl
Carving

Wildfowl Carving

Roger Schroeder

STACKPOLE
BOOKS

*To Dave and Mary, Phil, Martin, Grant, Jim, Peter, Leo,
Floyd, Greg, and Joan and Eugene
To my supportive wife, Sheila, who has a remarkable eye
for good bird sculpture
And to Bruce Burk, who has shown the way for nearly all
the carvers in this book, as well as thousands more.*

Copyright © 1992 by Stackpole Books

Published by
STACKPOLE BOOKS
Cameron and Kelker Streets
P.O. Box 1831
Harrisburg PA 17105

Interior design by Donna Mark Miller.

Photographs by Roger Schroeder unless otherwise credited.

Printed in the United States of America

10 9 8 7 6 5 4 3 2 1

Library of Congress Cataloging-in-Publication Data

Schroeder, Roger, 1945–
    Wildfowl carving / Roger Schroeder. — 1st ed.
        p.   cm.
    ISBN 0-8117-0867-5
    1. Wood-carving. 2. Birds in art. I. Title.
TT199.7.S4   1992
731'.832—dc20
                                        92-15229
                                        CIP

CONTENTS

Dave and Mary Ahrendt   1
Planes and Lines and Focal Points

Phil Galatas   25
Miniatures and More

Martin Gates   57
Hand Tools and Hardwoods

Grant Goltz   89
Theories of Design

Jim Hazeley   121
Vignetting

Peter Kaune   153
Capturing Essence

Leo Osborne   185
Art Without Limits

Floyd Scholz   217
Orchestrating Balance and Harmony

Greg Woodard   249
A Love for Raptors

Joan Zygmunt and Eugene Morelli   281
The Art of Balance

PREFACE

Interviews are easy affairs. I sit down with the carver, get him or her working, have a camera ready, and turn on the tape recorder. It's really as simple as that. One carver wanted to know in advance what questions I would be asking. I told him I travel light. I take only one question with me: How did you get started? All the rest come from that first answer and from what I see around the workshop, what the carver is working on.

Traveling around the country to get material for this book, I found each visit fascinating. I like meeting the carvers in their shops, getting to know them where they are most at ease. I like having them talk about their work while they are doing it. As we discussed design, painting, habitat, and the relationship of the bird to its environment, I could see how each carver makes it all happen.

Bringing together the material for *Wildfowl Carving* has been for me an exciting and instructive experience. I've sat at the elbows of some of the best bird carvers in the world and we've worked together to make a book that, we hope, captures the nature and spirit of their work.

Special thanks go to all those who helped: Marie Bongiovanni, Mike and Julia Kinsley, Charles Potter, Larry Stevens, Charles Warrington, and Barbara Gehrm and Donna Stalder of the Ward Foundation.

Roger Schroeder
Amityville, New York

Dave and Mary Ahrendt

*Planes and Lines
And Focal Points*

Dave and Mary Ahrendt work together on bird sculptures that are both impressionistic and realistic. Their birds emerge with remarkable energy and flair from pieces of wood rich in grain and color. Mary had taken an art course in college but had decided not to pursue art as a profession. Dave, on the other hand, had always dreamed of being an artist, but, he says, "I was embarrassed by my lack of artistic ability." His confidence grew as he pursued his hobbies—nature photography, taxidermy, and finally carving.

They began carving in 1981. Mary bought Dave a set of carving tools and a copy of Bruce Burk's *Game Bird Carving*. Dave worked through two projects from the book, a canvasback and a mallard, and Mary painted them. In 1983, after having carved only six or seven birds, they decided to carve full-time "and take our chances," Mary says. They left Alaska, where they had been teaching school in a remote Eskimo village, and returned to Minnesota. Together they built their house on Widow Lake, near Hackensack, two hundred miles from Minneapolis–St. Paul, and set up shop.

"We had no formal art training, so we tried to spend the first several years laying a broad foundation: learning the technical aspects as well as studying how a bird is put together. Later we started studying art and art principles—rules for why things look good."

They read books on design, visited art museums, and had other painters and sculptors critique their work. "There are reasons why certain things look good," Dave says, "and reasons why the eye moves along a piece." They started a notebook listing the principles of what they considered good art and tried to make their own realistic carvings conform to these principles.

During this period of concentrated study they decided they wanted to do something different. "To survive, we felt our work had to stand out, to be distinctly different," Dave says.

They were influenced by Morton Solberg, a California painter who specializes in North American wildlife. His work, which ranges from landscapes to vignettes, blends the realistic and the abstract. Solberg wants the viewer to experience the feeling of standing in a mountain stream or feeling mountain fog closing in around him. Dave and Mary were impressed by what they describe as "his loose, abstract backgrounds that give his paintings a sense of emotion."

Dave and Mary decided they wanted to apply Solberg's approach to wood. They began experimenting, creating sculptures in which the bird is realistic but the rest of the piece is abstract. They explain, "The key to success is not abstraction for the sake of abstraction. Instead, it is the need to create the impression of a specific feeling, like movement, speed, or power."

In 1987 they began their first impressionistic piece, a trio of cedar waxwings. Working in clay, they decided on a composition that would bring together an abstract walnut base with emerging, partially detailed birds. They wanted the abstraction to convey the motion of a feeding flock of birds and at the same time convey the essence of that particular species. "Our objective was to create movement in an excited flock of feeding birds about to descend on a berry tree and feed for ten to fifteen minutes and then be gone."

The piece took a best-in-show in the Yorkarvers Woodcarving and Decoy Show. "It opened our eyes," Dave remembers. "We realized that the piece had value. It won over realistic birds, something totally unexpected."

"In working with planes, we try to make smooth transitions between lines."

A preening dove done in 1989 is a piece that emphasizes the graceful form of a dove rather than its speed. The bird's turned head follows its body in an upward sweep that ends in the pointed tail. Rising up from behind the head and merging at the body near the tail is one wing. An open space between the wing and the body creates negative space and relieves some of the mass.

"We did not want to dead-end lines. If the lines are real hard, you end up with less transition. The way the back side of one wing and the tail come together on the dove is a good example of a smooth transition."

The surface of the wing is both convex and concave as it gently rolls and tapers into the body.

The primaries are slightly raised with no sharp lines, as are the secondaries and tertials. "At first we didn't carve in the tertials, but the piece lacked interest and was boring. You need certain numbers of stops so your eye doesn't move too quickly. A large plane with nothing happening, even one that is not flat, can be boring." When Dave and Mary carved in the tertials, they added an element that echoes the shape of the primaries and makes them stronger.

What makes the dove different from other pieces, aside from the emphasis on form, is that there is no texturing on the feathers. Paint alone creates the illusion of feathers.

A piece that is successful both in the use of diverse planes and in capturing the essence of a species is *Whitecap*. Done in 1988, the piece went through many transitions before it became wave and tern. The original model suggested a wave but did not include a seabird. Realizing they needed a water bird, Dave and Mary decided on a tern because it is typically found diving into the water, because its lines, they feel, are more pleasing than those of other birds, and because the bird's colors allowed them to keep the piece simple.

The tern's white body contrasts pleasingly with the dark wood, and the contrast promotes the sense of an emerging bird. They considered including a sunfish—typical prey—in the tern's orange beak. The colors worked together, but the shape of the sunfish interrupted the flow of the carving.

"The sunfish is round and flat. We needed something streamlined like a minnow. We tried to have an open mind with no pet notions or ideas that we wouldn't want to let go. We finally visualized the piece without the fish. We felt the piece was stronger if the minnow was implied. The diving tern says it. We didn't have to complete the story, and it took us one step closer to understatement. With one more element out of the picture, the focus is on the tern."

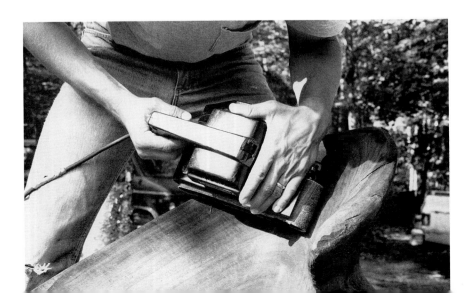

"The emphasis of our
work is on line and form."

For most of their impressionistic sculptures, the Ahrendts use American black walnut, the wood known as the perfect domestic cabinetmaker's wood. Not as heavy as oak and only medium-hard, walnut is still quite strong and works beautifully with hand and power tools. It ranges in color from a light tan to a rich purple-brown, is very stable, and does not tend to twist and warp.

Dave and Mary are attracted to walnut's dark color and rich grain, calling it a classical wood. "The wood grain, if used correctly, will enhance the perception of movement. But since the emphasis of our work is on line and form, we don't want the grain to dominate. Therefore we often wet-sand with Watco Danish Oil and 600-grit sandpaper to darken the piece and tame the grain."

Dave and Mary use a variety of lines and planes to imply movement and to make their sculptures interesting. They feel that flat surfaces are boring, so they often create concave or convex areas in their sculptures. In working with planes, the Ahrendts want the transitions between them to be smooth. The line, where two planes meet, can be made by undercutting or raising areas, such as feather groups, or by creating negative spaces.

"Our goal in this carving, *Berry Picker*, was quite simply to use a minimum of form and line and yet create the feeling of a feeding waxwing. We wanted to cut as much away as possible and still have the piece make a statement."

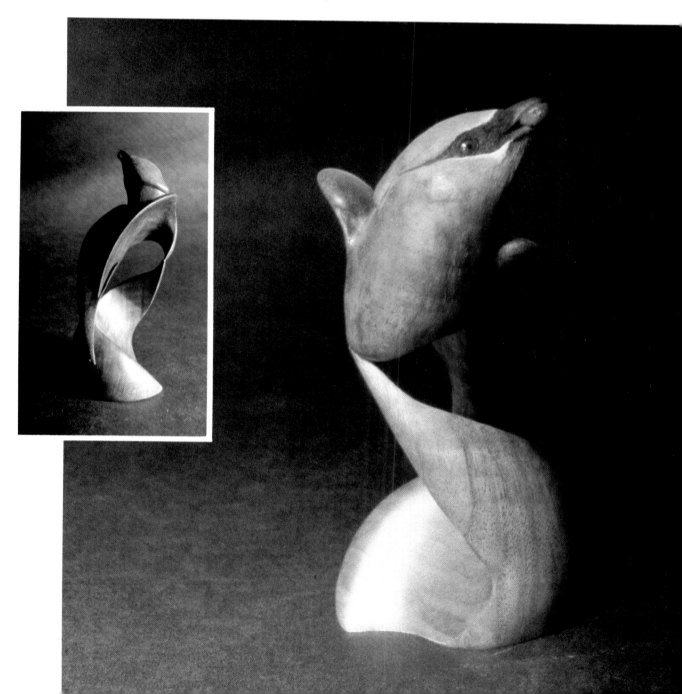

One for the Road, an American robin carved from black walnut, is a study in faceted planes and straight lines. Even the bird is in straight, horizontal flight. "This piece is a departure for us. It's quite different from our normal style, which consists of concave and convex planes and curving lines.

"The bird could have been any one of a number of species. In fact, we chose the robin late in the project, well after the sculpture was defined."

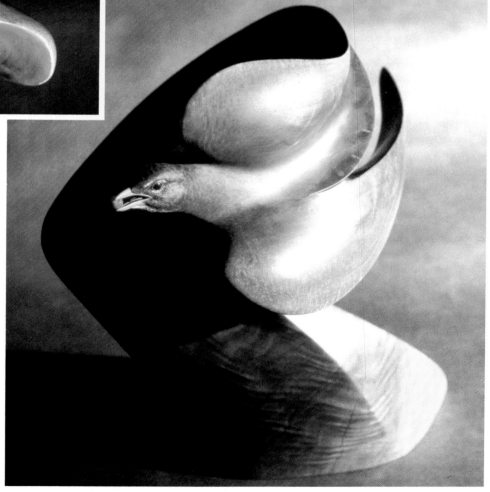

The berry helps tell a story.

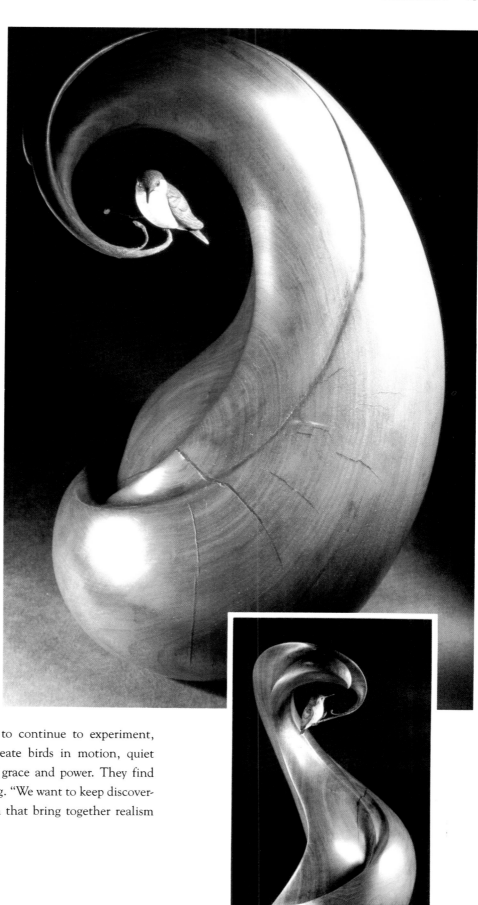

"Although good art is governed by many rules and principles, sometimes by deliberately breaking a rule exciting things happen."

"An accepted although unstated rule within the carving world is that the base should not compete with or overpower the bird." *Resting Jewel* features a realistic hummingbird, which as a design element is only an accent point. The dominating element, many times the size of the hummingbird, is a free-form walnut sculpture. This flowing sculpture features an important negative space within which the tiny bird rests. The energy from the large, abstract shape is directed to this negative space, and all the planes and lines lead the eye into this focal point.

Dave and Mary want to continue to experiment, sometimes by breaking rules, to create birds in motion, quiet birds, aggressive birds, and birds of grace and power. They find exploring and experimenting exciting. "We want to keep discovering new approaches to this art form that bring together realism and impressionism."

The Ahrendts had one goal with this piece from the onset: to create a quiet, oval shape and a quiet bird with its head tucked in. Mary began her exploration of color with this piece. She wanted to bring the black surface to life by adding other colors—blues and purples to mention a few.

"The piece evolved. We tried different birds and settled on the Canada goose." The piece, done in 1990 and titled *Canadian Quiescence,* is black walnut and stands nine inches high.

With *The Graceful One*, as the title implies, Dave and Mary wanted to portray gracefulness. The mourning dove, with its long wings and tail, is the perfect bird for this quiet, peaceful presentation.

"We liked the overall sculptural shape, the way its wings and tail meet and blend together, and the colors. The subtle blues, pinks, and reds were the sparks that brought zip to this piece."

A piece that started out as a walnut log six feet long and four feet in diameter went through many changes. The original concept was to have a peregrine falcon chasing bobwhite quail in a horizontal format using two different types of wood. The peregrine would have been sculpted in walnut, the quail in a burl of southwestern wood called mesquite. However, the two types of wood were not compatible. They went on to finish the quail piece and titled it *Broken Covey*.

When returning to the large, rough, chain-sawed walnut many months later, the Ahrendts could still see a large bird of prey banking around one end and chasing a group of birds. They worked many months on the wood before finally committing themselves to a sculpture of the largest falcon, a gyrfalcon, in pursuit of Arctic terns.

From their observations of this falcon, they decided to title the piece *Arctic Tail Chase*.

"A significant aspect of this work is that it shows the typical way a gyrfalcon captures its prey: not by stooping like a peregrine but by chasing and overtaking."

Three bobwhite quail emerge from a free-form piece of mesquite burl. Dave and Mary left most of the sculpture in its natural, weathered state, but they ran a line of finished wood down the snag-shaped piece. From the finished wood emerge three quail. Their wings and heads are detailed and painted and give direction to the birds.

"This was the first time a unique piece of wood stimulated an idea. The mesquite burl said 'quail.' It implied the plumage of bobwhite quail both in color and in pattern, and we could see, or guess might be a better word, the shapes of three birds. We skipped our usual clay model and went directly to the wood."

The color of the wood dictated a distinctive color pattern, and the zigzagging grain gave the impression of zigzagging flight.

"Why did we leave so much of the wood in its natural state? We felt the grays of the uncarved wood would contrast with the streaking flight of the birds, and too much finished wood would have overpowered the flying quail."

Two of the quail are female, one male; the sex differences provide contrast. The male is a darker brown than the females, and the females have a more directioned flight.

"Pieces of art need to create tension, but push it too far and the viewer is uncomfortable. It works best when a piece takes a viewer to the edge but doesn't push the viewer over. The edge itself is exciting."

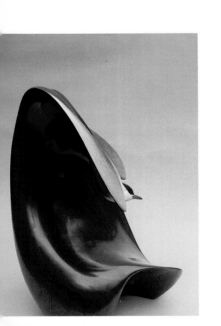

The base of *Whitecap* is relatively small. Dave and Mary wanted to avoid a heavy, massive feeling. A white bird emerges from a breaking wave of rich brown walnut. The wave is sculptural and implied rather than exact. It moves the bird along because the viewer knows what a breaking wave does and completes the picture on his own.

Dave and Mary first made a smaller sculpture of *Whitecap*, only ten inches high, one they describe as a study model. They lost momentum with the study and were at a point where they were tired of working on the piece. "The spontaneity was gone and it was hard to have an open mind when we got to the final sculpture because we were only trying to duplicate the smaller one."

"The realistic areas show the emerging nature of the birds and help direct the eye and imply movement. The fact that the front of the bird is real implies realism and makes the entire bird real."

Waxwing Invasion suggests a circular composition of three birds emerging from a piece of walnut. The piece conveys a great deal of motion as each bird twists its natural wood body. The lowest and uppermost birds have berries in their mouths. What is given detail are the heads and shoulders of the birds, each burned and painted. They are the focal points of the composition.

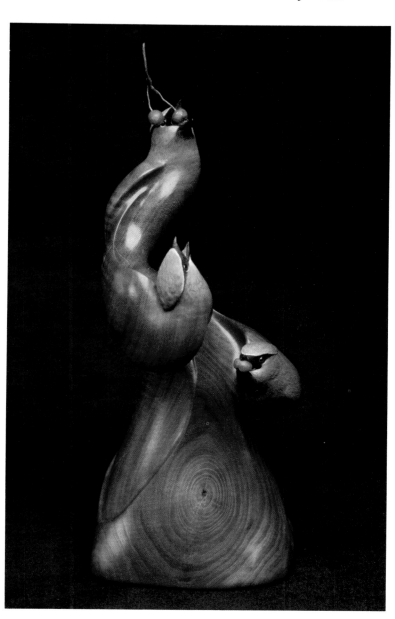

Dave and Mary did not sculpt the composition from a single piece of walnut. Instead they carved the heads from a different kind of wood. "We were of the opinion that if you do something in detail, you need a wood that you can texture." They chose to carve the heads in tupelo. Later they discovered that walnut also textures well, taking an even finer texture than tupelo. This is the last piece in which they incorporate separate pieces of wood.

"One wing dissolves into another wing, or a wing dissolves into a body line. We were very aware of placing the three birds so that they were not equally spaced. We wanted the three birds doing very different things."

Dave and Mary decided to carve a large piece for the 1988 World Championships. They chose a peregrine falcon stooping on a swallow, the medium to be walnut. Wanting to do a composition for the World Class, they asked themselves what bird would have the greatest impact on people, and they decided on the peregrine. The next questions were: What captures the essence of a peregrine, and what could it be doing that people would relate to? Dave says, "People feel the peregrine is the master of the air. So a stooping or diving bird was our answer."

The next step was deciding on the presentation. They felt an impressionistic one that conveyed speed and power was more important than a realistic rendering. They made a model that successfully implied both speed and power, but, they admit, it also said "water," something people would not associate with the peregrine. So they set that model aside.

They kept working and eventually decided they wanted to create a chase: peregrine stooping on a swallow. The fear and helplessness of the prey, they decided, would be a minor element in the composition. Ultimately all their design decisions focused on what would make the falcon faster and more powerful.

Dave made a number of clay models and Mary critiqued them. Dave says, "Mary provides a different perspective. When you work closely with a sculpture, you don't always see things objectively." They finally agreed to use a swallow as prey.

Why did they choose a swallow? Their first choice had been a swift, a classic matchup of two of the fastest birds in the world. But the Ahrendts knew that wildlife painter Robert Bateman had done a chase scene with a peregrine and a swift, and they, as ever, were looking to create something different. The coloring of the swallow swayed them. Its blues are compatible with those of the falcon, while the browns of the swift would have been lost in the walnut.

The peregrine and swallow piece has a great number of convex or concave surfaces. The undetailed wings of the peregrine sweep back and up, as do the unpainted body and tail. The wood between the falcon and swallow complements the shape of the peregrine while offering negative space that breaks up the mass of the piece. Emerging out of the transitional wood is the swallow, the body and one wing of which blends and twists in retreat.

The Ahrendts wanted the color of *The Scarlet Tanager* to contrast with the sculptural shape from which it is emerging. The bird's color helps it stand out from the black walnut. "We fade bright color into the base, a treatment that we feel helps imply movement and a sense of emerging.

"We approached the *Crimson Spiral* with a goal of exploring a geometric shape—the spiral—which, by its very nature, implies movement. Any number of birds would have worked, but we chose the cardinal because its crest is so interesting and it gave us a nice line where we needed it."

"We want to explore the tactile aspect of wood sculpture."

Resting is one of Dave and Mary's favorite pieces. They feel it successfully captures the nature of a sleeping tern. When they first began to conceive the design, they wanted to create a sculptural shape that "felt good to hold."

This piece is six inches long, done in black walnut. The Ahrendts textured the wood, a technique they think works for this piece.

Phil Galatas

*Miniatures
And More*

Growing up on Bayou Liberty in southern Louisiana, Phil Galatas lived in a home that did not have a telephone until he was eight or a car until he was in high school. Boats took the place of cars, and Phil spent time out in a pirogue exploring the bayou. His father was a hunter, trapper, and fisherman, and Phil, as a child, learned about nature and wildlife.

Art interested him as well, and Phil made drawings of outdoor settings. Once he painted a swamp scene and sold it to a neighbor for eight dollars. Phil left the bayou to attend Delgado College, where he earned a commercial art degree and decided upon graduation in 1970 to become a full-time artist. Much of his early work is devoted to wildlife themes.

In 1976 Phil went to a carving competition in New Orleans with a cousin who was entering decoys. Phil remembers seeing an animated piece, a peregrine falcon descending on a pintail duck while another pintail jumped from a marsh. It was the work of two brothers, Charles and Rudy Hutchinson, who carved in their spare time. John Viola, Lynn Forehand, and Tan Brunet have also influenced Phil.

Phil entered his first show, the Gulf South Championship, in 1977 with a pair of flying green-winged teal. He put them in the open, or professional, division and took a first in decorative miniature waterfowl and a second-in-show. "Once you win a blue ribbon, you're all excited and it gets to be addictive."

In 1986 Phil began thinking about carving a Canada goose in flight. Shortly before attending the Eastern Waterfowl Festival, he saw on the cover of *Sports Afield* a Canada goose coming in for a landing on water. He also remembers seeing Canada geese flying overhead during the show. "It was a cold, cloudy day, and the geese set the mood."

Each year a carver is chosen to do a piece for display in the lobby of Easton's Tidewater Inn. Jim Sprankle had already been chosen to do the featured carving for the Tidewater Inn in 1988. Phil was called in by the committee and asked to do a flying Canada goose for the 1989 festival.

Phil began the project by drawing a goose's anatomy, taking measurements of a specimen, and doing patterns of feather layouts. He found a good mounted bird for color reference and was ready to start carving by early December 1988. He ordered three pieces of tupelo from Curt Fabre: one measuring twelve inches square by thirty inches long for the body, the other two measuring seven inches by twelve inches by forty-eight inches for the wings. When the wood arrived, he realized the enormity of the undertaking.

Phil began not with the body but with the head and neck, which were to be separate pieces. He shaped these with his grinding tools. When he came to the wings, he did the roughing out with

gouges and a hatchet. He had not worked previously with gouges because he felt they would remove wood more quickly than rotary tools. He had the hatchet custom made with a curved blade and an edge that went around the front. "It looks like a comma with a handle on it. Only one side was beveled. It's like an adze, but it's used like a hatchet. The design keeps the edge from binding."

Once he became comfortable with the hand tools, he went to work on the body with gouges and chisels. He found he enjoyed using them because they do not produce the dust that grinding tools spew out.

Phil put off work on the wings and feathers until

he had completed the habitat. He did not texture the wings, but instead burned in all the shaft and barb lines. Phil guesses he made seven thousand burn lines on the first ten primaries. Multiply that number by four to account for the two sides of both wings, then do the same for the secondaries. He feels now that it was a mistake to burn the wings and wishes he had used more texturing lines. Except for the scapulars and tail feathers, he did texture the body.

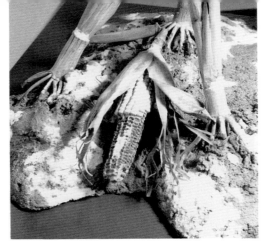

Phil had brought some cornstalks back from Easton. Some corncobs on the stalks, damaged in harvesting, had the winter-field look he wanted. Playing with ideas for how to mount the goose, Phil placed the stalks upright on a large scrap piece of tupelo.

He decided to suspend the goose by one foot and use a cornstalk to hold it in place. To design a suspension system that would hold eighteen pounds of wood, he ran a steel rod measuring a half inch square through the center of the cornstalk that was carved of tupelo, cut in half, and routed in the center. To secure the piece, he welded the bottom of the rod to a quarter-inch-thick iron plate.

Phil feared the suspended goose and the cornfield base might be too heavy to move easily, so he decided to lighten the base. Taking a three-quarter-inch piece of plywood, he added chicken wire to create the mounds that make up corn rows. He stapled the wire to the plywood and filled the spaces between the plywood and wire with a spray insulation foam, shaving off the excess.

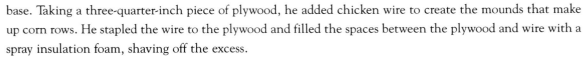

To make the cornhusks, Phil used brass shim stock. By nailing a piece down and scoring it with a pick to make the ridges, he found that it rolled up like a cigar when he removed the nails. Phil frayed the edges with a grinder, made holes for the husks in the stalks, and epoxied them in place.

He primed the brass with Rustoleum the color of raw sienna, which he painted over. He wanted to use a color closest to the final color so that if any of the base coat showed through, it would not be a problem.

To make Maryland-like dirt, a friend sent him samples. Phil used a mix of Bondo auto body filler and sawdust to match them. He mixed the Bondo and sawdust together before adding the hardening agent and used a putty knife to push the dirt into the chicken wire. "It left a rough texture like crumbled dirt." He stippled the hardened Bondo and sawdust with raw sienna, raw umber, burnt sienna, a fast-drying white, and some black.

For one final touch—a look of snow on the ground and on some of the stalks—Phil used an adhesive flocking material.

"I wanted to capture a northwest or northeast cliff scene, one close to the coast. I put a lot of lichen on the rocks, and made an old, weathered, twisted, gnarled tree. But I wanted to keep the bird away from the habitat."

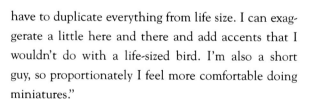

Phil intended to carve a life-sized peregrine falcon, but because he wanted to enter the piece in the 1989 World Championships, he had little time. He decided to carve a miniature piece: a falcon perched far out on a tree that emerges from rocks. Much of Phil's work is in miniature scale. Miniature compositions sell faster than full-sized pieces and take less time to complete. "My patience is short. The machines and my hands won't produce fast enough. Working on a miniature scale, I can get the same shape as a life-sized piece and get it out of my system. A miniature may not have the same grandeur, but it's really a smaller version of a large piece that can drag on for as long as ten months.

"There are other advantages to doing miniatures. Miniature pieces are easy to hold, and I can take shortcuts with design. I don't have to duplicate everything from life size. I can exaggerate a little here and there and add accents that I wouldn't do with a life-sized bird. I'm also a short guy, so proportionately I feel more comfortable doing miniatures."

Phil designed the bird with its tail swept to one side. He wanted to create the illusion of bird bracing against the wind. "I can see the tension. That's one reason why I think the composition works."

The piece is titled *Watch On* because the falcons soar high in the air and watch for their prey's movement and flashes of color.

For the World Show of 1990 Phil had planned to enter two compositions: one for the decorative life-sized division, one for the miniature division. "But a friend told me to put my efforts into just one, not to sacrifice one piece to make two. I listened and made *Highlands Defender*. It won Best-in-World Decorative Miniature."

Phil has the hawk standing in a mantling position on a stump, rocks around the wood. "I wanted to set the piece in the highlands, above the tree line where only a hiker might go. People ask me why I have the bird mantling without prey under it and why the bird is protectively spreading its wings. The bird is really mantling its environment, which is why I titled the piece *Highlands Defender*. I did not want to do a piece with prey. Ladies don't like dead, dangling things."

"I am particularly fond of the redtail. It's a versatile bird of prey, a ferocious, aggressive bird that can soar, move fast, and eat just about anything. I like its striking, large, red tail."

PHOTOGRAPHS ON PAGES 34 TO 39 BY PHIL GALATAS

Phil wanted to do a bird of prey for the Gulf South Championship in 1990. According to the rules, he had to have two subjects: predator and prey, or male and female birds. He wanted to do a small bird of prey, but ruled out the kestrel because he felt too many were being done. He finally decided on a merlin.

Phil took measurements of the raptor from a museum specimen and talked with a falconer who works at the Science and Nature Center in New Orleans to learn about the bird. Before he started the composition, Phil worked out a color scheme that would complement the blue-grays and buff colors of the merlin. He decided to place the bird on a gray rock. The bird and rock are carved from a single piece of tupelo.

"The base of the composition could not be a traditional walnut turning because I wanted a blue-gray and buff color scheme. I tried a dark gray base, but without success. I could have achieved the perfect color through natural bleaching if I could have let the wood sit out in the sun, but I didn't have the time."

"The base is cedar, which I turned, sandblasted, and painted. But I was not satisfied, so I ended up staining the wood."

After band sawing the outline, Phil used gouges to define the shape. Phil drew and redrew the feather layout many times during the initial roughing out. He used a half-inch shallow gouge to define the feather groups and a three-quarter-inch-by-one-inch sanding drum to shape the right primaries and tail feathers.

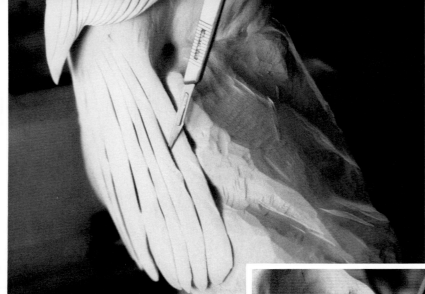

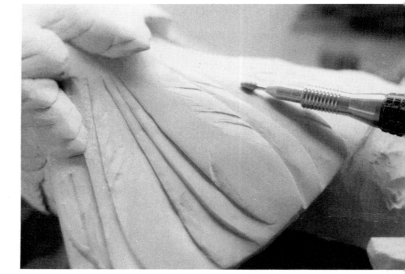

I f he's doing a hooked beak, Phil inserts a piece of sharpened stainless
steel wire into the tip of the beak after he drills the hole. He builds up
the area with a drop of Bondo, a material used for auto body repair,
and then shapes the tip. "I've found this makes for a tip that's real sharp and
real hard."

The wing feathers are laid out, ready for cutting with knives.
Phil adds wood to the front of the composition so that the merlin will appear
balanced at the top of a sloping rock. The tail remains connected to the rock
and is undercut slightly. Phil uses a scalpel to under-
cut the tail feathers and a diamond bit to add more
shape. He removes the right primaries so the tail is
more accessible.

Doing research for the piece, Phil discovered that merlins follow warblers during their migration from the mountains north where he lived to the Gulf of Mexico. He put a yellow-rumped warbler in the merlin's talons.

On the warbler Phil uses knives, a half-inch-diameter sanding drum, and an eighth-inch-diameter diamond cylinder to give detail. He textures feathers with an eighth-inch-diameter diamond bit and fits the warbler into place. He'll fit the toes of the merlin later. He places rocks made from tupelo and uses sawdust to simulate earth.

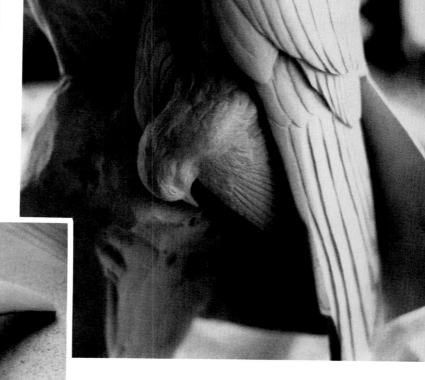

"Doing a dead songbird was new to me. Usually I try to catch the life of a bird, and this time I had to create a dead one."

After the birds and rock were completed, Phil felt the composition was lacking. "It didn't have the height. So I worked with the pieces of wood and added a branch that twines around and up the piece. Once the branch was in place, I felt the piece looked fine. I wanted the piece to be viewed from any angle. That was the biggest challenge."

Phil uses an eighth-inch-diameter diamond bit for the texture and splits and burns in the quills. He textures and paints the rocks and then attaches them to the base with Bondo. The branch, carved from tupelo, completes the composition.

Phil ended up working on the piece right through the early morning on the day of the show. He slept for an hour, and when his wife woke him for registration, she said, "You're a magician. You finished it." Galatas decided to title the piece *Little Magician*. "These birds fluff up and look bigger than they really are. That makes them magicians as well."

In 1990 *The Little Magician* earned Phil his third Gulf South Championship.

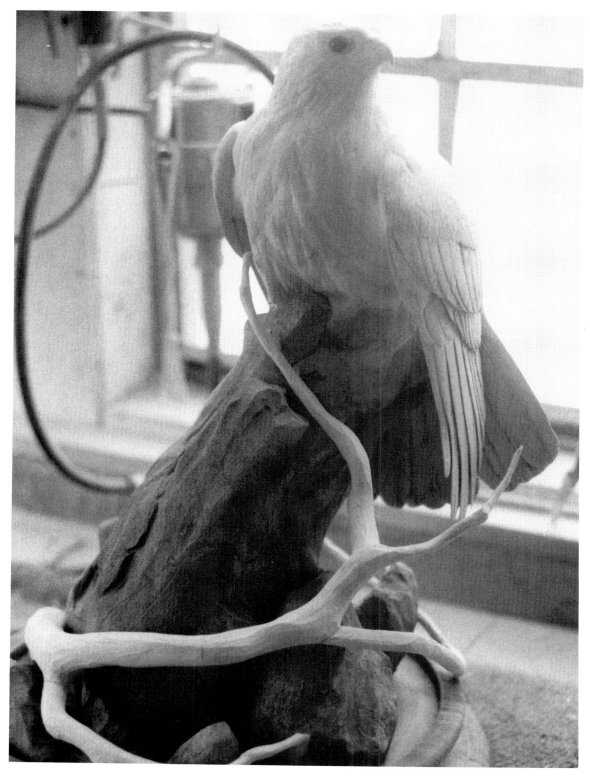

"I wanted an expression in the face that says, 'I got the songbird so I don't have to look at it. But I'll look around and protect my prey.' That's what I was after."

Sketch of ospreys and
crappie that will one day be
a miniature sculpture.

PHOTOGRAPHS ON PAGES 41 TO 49
BY BILL WARNER

The goose is painted in oils. For the habitat, Phil used fast-drying oils, but on the bird he wanted the paint to stay damp as long as possible while he blended areas. "Acrylics dry too quickly. I like oils, the way they blend, the softness and the richness of their colors. Some carvers can do wonders with acrylics, but I still see a little bit of the synthetic look with them."

" I did mostly dry brushing on the goose, working in as many highlights and shadows as I could to bring it alive, especially the undersides of the wings." Phil even added colors like red, which he does not normally use, to emphasize certain areas.

To paint the wings, he mounted each one on a three-foot-by-four-foot drawing table adjusted to a vertical position. He had to stand to paint the wings but felt it was easier to blend the colors this way, especially on feathers as large as the ones he carved.

Ballet on the Wind won first-in-category and second-in-show in open class decorative life size at the World Championships.

Phil placed the goose and habitat on a pedestal measuring twenty-three inches square by thirty-six inches high. Instead of painting the pedestal black, he applied black formica to the sides. *Ballet on the Wind* stands nearly seven feet high.

When the editor of *Wildfowl Carving and Collecting* magazine asked Phil to do a two-part article on carving and painting, he decided that a flying mallard would make a good project. The piece took several months to complete because he had to work with a writer who was documenting and photographing each technique.

"I don't do a piece like this with the intensity that I apply to a competition piece, but I do a good job. I admit that I was afraid I was not going to come out with a piece that was good enough for the readers."

To keep the piece simple, Phil mounted the mallard on a piece of driftwood and used a simple suspension system. "I have seen several projects done by carvers who followed my step-by-step instructions, and I am pleased with their results."

Flying Wigeon is a piece Phil wanted to do for some time. He had seen only one other carved wigeon in flight, a minia-ture, and thought it was beautiful. Phil wanted to do a full-sized bird, and as he be-gan work on the pattern of the piece, a New Orleans physician agreed to commission it.

When Phil was ready to deliver the carving, the doctor had passed away, so Phil kept the piece and entered it in a Ducks Unlimited exhibition. "I would not do a rump mount again, but I was experimenting, using tubing for the suspension.

"This was my first try at a fly-ing bird, and it really got me ready for *Ballet on the Wind*."

"The three birds face no threat,
have nothing to excite them.
They're on their own in a marsh,
doing what ducks do: sleeping,
stretching, preening, and fighting."

Phil likes the composition of three birds. He agrees with an art teacher who taught him that, in design, odd numbers work better than even ones. "Three balances things out and fills out the space." These canvasbacks, done in 1982, were among Phil's first experiments with three-bird compositions. He exhibited them at a National Wildlife Federation competition in Washington, D.C., in 1984. It was the first time he was competing against two world champions, Larry Barth and William Koelpin, and he remembers the experience vividly. "It inspired me and got me fired up. I said to myself, 'I'll be a world champion sooner or later if I put my time in.'"

Phil's first entry at the World Championships was *Three Gadwalls*. He decided to do these three ducks in a typical Louisiana marsh setting. "I wanted to bring the piece to the World and knock 'em dead, so I took my time with the detail work. The preening female was done as one piece. Another duck is walking, and a third is drying its wings. I didn't place with the birds—my first taste of defeat."

Mallard Pair was one of Phil's early miniature pieces. "I had been carving decoys and putting them in environmental settings. I used colored resin and marsh grass made from split bamboo. As I look back now, the piece seems so plain."

At the time, he was experimenting with bases, using mahogany because he could not purchase walnut. In the resin, he used liquid stain, the kind used in making stained glass. He got the bamboo from an old bird cage. Taking the cage apart, he split the bamboo with a scalpel and shaved the pieces so they separated without coming off of the stick. The grass looked good and was durable. Today, he uses metals for this kind of habitat.

The three miniature gadwalls won best-in-show at the Louisiana Wildfowl Festival in 1984.

The mouth of the redtail is open. "I shaped the outside of the open beak and left wood between the mandibles. Then I drew the opening and made a light cut around it. I worked on the body, the wings, and the habitat and left the open mouth until last. I was going to insert a tongue, but the last time I did that, John Scheeler said it looked like a toothpick. So I carved the mouth with the tongue in place."

PHOTOGRAPHS ON PAGES 51 TO 56 BY ROGER SCHROEDER

Phil did three separate bases before he decided on one that has broad, sweeping sides, especially on the front. "The mantling position lends itself to a circular design. The angles on the base definitely affect the bird. The base flares out and up in such a way that energy flows from the base to the bird. I wanted power coming like an imaginary line through the body and out of the head."

Phil's first major piece was *Mourning Dove*. The compositions of John James Audubon influenced the design. "I experimented with spread wings and wire feet. I used bamboo for the grass and carved pine cones and pine chips. The base is teak wood."

This piece took second-in-show at the 1979 Gulf South Championship.

Phil began this piece with the base, and he tried four different bases before he found one he liked. "Once I had the design I wanted, the bird fell into place. The peregrine is only five and a half inches tall, while the entire piece stands at thirteen inches."

"I wanted the viewer to be able to look at the bird without being influenced by the base, as if they are independent of each other."

"The bird is not looking at the viewer. It's as if the viewer isn't even there. This is a wild bird, alone, untouchable, and isolated out there with no effects of mankind on him. I feel what is particularly striking about the piece is the force that comes through the bird's eyes. You're seeing the world through those eyes. I wanted to achieve a sense of motion from the base to the bird. It's important to get a sense of motion, a flow from the base, and have all that built-up energy come out at the bird as if the energy is being sucked up out of the base."

Phil finished the composition one week before the World Championships, satisfied that it was a special piece and a successful one.

Not all of Phil's compositions are energetic. Some are simple, sedate pieces featuring birds in quiet poses. In *Swamp Emeralds* two miniature wood ducks rest in a pond setting. The drake is centered. Duckweed and iris grow in resinous water. Phil designed this piece from the top making two ovals and drawing a base around them. He finished the piece in a month but spent more than two hundred hours on it, working up until the morning of the 1989 Louisiana Wildfowl Festival Gulf South Championship. The wood ducks won the competition.

Martin Gates

*Hand Tools
And Hardwoods*

Martin Gates received his early training in wood and tools from his father whose business was antiques. Martin's father liked to go to Europe in search of quality pieces, and he brought back pearwood cabinets, French armoires, and sculpture for Martin to work on. Martin admired the streamlined, geometric art deco pieces and thinks his carvings have an art deco quality to them.

Martin tried wood carving when he was fifteen. "I was staying at my grandparents' cabin in the mountains. I was attracted to wood and familiar with it, so the natural place for me to hang out was the wood pile. I picked out a nice piece of juniper and, with my granddad's carpenter chisel and claw hammer, carved an Indian head."

His first exposure to bird carving was years later in 1972 when he got a copy of Bruce Burk's *Game Bird Carving*. He was living in Maryland at the time and thinks he might have been bitten by the decoy bug. He did one project from the book, a bufflehead, the only bird he has ever painted. He found he preferred natural wood.

Wanting to become a better carver and do better restoration work in his father's store, in 1976 he enrolled in the John C. Campbell Folk School in Brasstown, North Carolina. More than 3,000 students from all over the country attend the school's 350 classes each year. Though many native crafts are taught, wood carving is the mainstay and the most popular.

At the Campbell Folk School Martin carved a mule, a donkey, a duck, and the head of a carousel horse. "I loved sitting there all day long whittling, and I thought it would be great to do that for a living. I also learned to appreciate folk figures done by European carvers, the kind my father brought back from his buying trips to Europe. When you look at what was made by carvers who studied their trade for years, you come to appreciate that they carved throughout their lives and worked up unique designs."

Martin credits Dan DeMendoza, a fellow Floridian and nationally known bird carver, with teaching him the basics of anatomy and feather patterns. "Birds, unlike other animals or even human figures, offer an infinite range of possibilities for the carver. My mind just goes crazy with ideas for wildfowl sculpture."

When Martin entered and won Best-in-World, Interpretive Wood Sculpture, at the 1987 World Championship Wildfowl Carving Competition, his father decided that he should carve full-time and fired him from the antiques store. Martin is not at all unhappy. "After I won the World Championship, I knew I didn't want to wait until I retired to carve full-time."

"I try to match the wood to the duck. Pintails look best made of walnut, and canvasbacks look best in cherry."

" 've always liked the beauty of wood, and for years I've collected wood from many sources." When Martin traveled out of state to deliver antiques for his father, he would bring back logs. Many of his early works, as well as some recent pieces, are waterfowl done in walnut and cherry wood, the hardwoods he prefers for their color and grain.

Martin's ducks are not one-piece sculptures. The head, neck, and tail are separate pieces. The tail is made as a wedge and inserted into the rump.

Rather than leave the body smooth, Martin carves in feather groupings and gives them strong definition. "A pintail has pretty feathers with interesting shapes. You can identify a duck by its feathers, especially the tertials, so I incorporate them as part of the design."

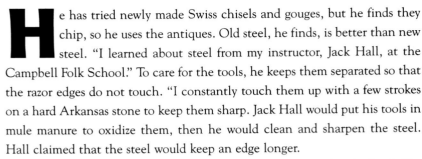

Martin prefers hand tools. "The cutters on rotary tools overheat, especially if you're working with hardwoods. Rotary tools chip if you change direction in grain and cutting depth."

He has tried newly made Swiss chisels and gouges, but he finds they chip, so he uses the antiques. Old steel, he finds, is better than new steel. "I learned about steel from my instructor, Jack Hall, at the Campbell Folk School." To care for the tools, he keeps them separated so that the razor edges do not touch. "I constantly touch them up with a few strokes on a hard Arkansas stone to keep them sharp. Jack Hall would put his tools in mule manure to oxidize them, then he would clean and sharpen the steel. Hall claimed that the steel would keep an edge longer.

"The tool I am most fond of for removing wood is the knife. For hardwood I need a thin-bladed knife with a long bevel on the cutting edge. The knife acts like a wedge and forces the wood apart. Without it, you'll crush the grain. With a wood like cherry, you can't pry it away. You have to slice it.

"I hold the blade flat to the wood because it is easier to get the knife to follow a straight line, and I have more surface to control. The knife acts like a rudder.

"You have to be patient with cherry. It is so tight and close grained. But it cuts cleanly with hand tools, and it's good for carving details because it has such straight grain.

"Walnut is not as consistently hard as cherry— some pieces are hard, some are soft. But it has more variety of color than cherry. Walnut will range from greenish brown to light brown to purplish red, depending on the minerals in the soil.

"I also worked with sycamore, also known as buttonwood, plane tree, and water beech. A sycamore tree can grow as high as one hundred sixty feet and have a diameter of up to five feet. The sapwood is light tan to reddish brown. I find flecking in the wood pretty, and I like finding old tools made from sycamore. It's a tight-grained wood and medium-hard like maple. I prefer the creamy white color."

Martin also carves wormy chestnut. American chestnut was versatile and popular among American woodworkers, but a blight brought from Asia in 1904 wiped out the tree by the 1930s. Large pieces of chestnut can still be found, but they are usually filled with worm holes. "Chestnut finishes nicely, but cutting across the grain is difficult because it has hard and soft spots. It's like cutting across yellow pine. For chestnut I use a thin-bladed knife, even one as small as an X-acto."

Martin also works in mahogany. Used as a cabinetmaking wood by European colonists since the sixteenth century, it is favored for its fine grain, firmness, and durability.

Martin first learned about the World Championships in February 1987 and had only two months to complete a piece for the competition. He had observed wading birds at a fish camp on Florida's Cross Creek and decided to sculpt a snowy egret.

For wood Martin used a log of West Indian mahogany that he found on the bank of the Suawanoe River. Because the log had some rotten spots, Martin worked out a plan to avoid the bad wood by putting the bird in a more vertical position than he had initially planned. The log was about six feet long and eighteen inches in diameter at the butt end. Part of it was rotten and the outside was heavily weathered, but within three-quarters of an inch under that surface he found most of the wood both workable and attractive.

He created patterns made of brown wrapping paper and taped them to the log, working out problems of dimensions and composition before removing any wood.

Using a chain saw to flatten the bottom of the log so it would rest easily on his workbench, Martin roughed out the piece. But he did not bring the wood down to a near-finished size. "I make rough cuts with the chain saw. I don't do a lot of refining with it. I leave room for some changes or problems I might run into with the wood." As he worked on the mahogany log, he discovered a knot where the egret's bill was to be. With plenty of log left, he was able to alter the design, change the area of wood he was removing, and turn the head.

Martin uses a number of rasps, surform tools, rifflers, and files. A favorite rasp of his is a Nicholson No. 50. "It makes such smooth cuts, I hardly need to sand if I run it in one direction." When Martin is working with gouges, the sculpture is not anchored down. Instead, he uses his body, feet, and knees to hold it in place. Often Martin keeps details simple because many times the wood is rotten or the grain is figured and he needs to be able to adapt his design. After he achieves the final anatomical shape, he uses scrapers and sandpaper for the finishing touches.

As Martin removes wood from the large pieces, he often must deal with the cracks that result from the drying process. "I'll fill the cracks with individual strips of wood, what I call mosaic fillings. I'll take chips off the floor and insert them. I'll make lots of small wedges instead of using a solid strip or wedge that would attract the eye to a rough line."

For small cracks, he makes a paste from dust built up by wet sanding the wood with linseed oil and turpentine. He prefers to use a cloth-backed Swiss sanding cloth because it does not crease or fall apart. He lets the paste build up in the cracks and applies a gap filler called Zap to the paste. The Zap soaks in and hardens the paste.

He does not like to use coarse sawdust from the floor or dust collected in a belt sander bag, which might be contaminated by wood particles from other species.

At one time Martin finished his wood with tung oil, but now he uses Watco Natural Danish Oil, an oil and resin finish. "The Watco oil is thinner, making it easier to apply, and it has greater penetration than the tung oil, which is thicker and more like syrup." He applies three or four coats of the Watco oil, rubbing with 0000 steel wool between applications, and finally a coat of paste wax.

"This was the hardest wood I'd ever worked. And with the reversing direction of the grain, I had to do a lot of rasping and sanding."

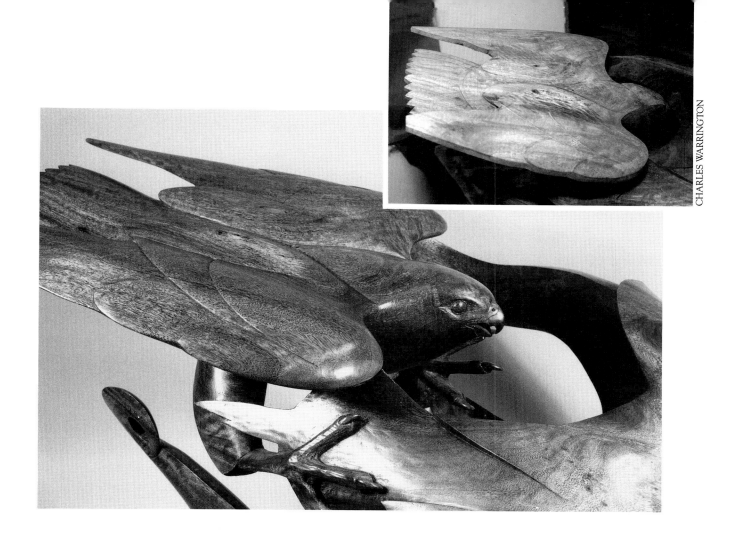

CHARLES WARRINGTON

In February 1988 Martin began a project in mahogany, a peregrine falcon attacking a canvasback duck in flight. He chose a log approximately eighteen by twenty-two by thirty-six inches. The wood had burl and tiger-stripe figuring and crotch wood where the tree had forked. He had to fit the birds to the medium. "This kind of wood makes it difficult to do detailed work. A figured surface doesn't lend it-self to a lot of details."

As he began removing wood, he came across another prob-lem—an excess of punky or soft wood. He had to change from a canvasback to a pintail because the pintail has a slim-mer breast and would fit better in the good wood that remained.

Martin designed the sculpture so the duck would have a chance to escape from the peregrine by disappearing into the cloud below. "The duck's form does not reflect the animation I was after, and I didn't have enough good wood left to accommodate a turned or raised head. But I feel I used the wedge-shaped log to my advantage. I carved the birds diving downward at great speed, and I am pleased with the results."

He decided not to use Watco oil for the finish but applied Deft lacquer first with a brush and then with an aerosol can. "It would have taken too many coats of Watco to harden on the surface. Deft is the best lacquer on the market, and it dries within twenty minutes."

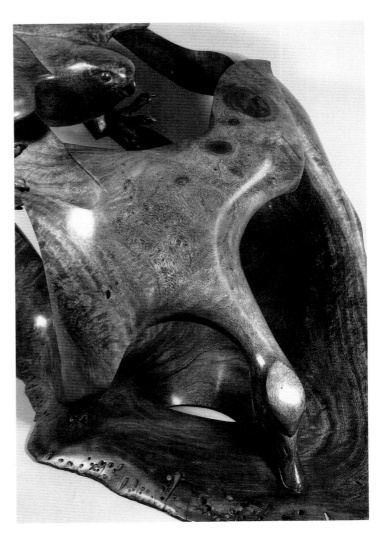

"I wanted to direct the viewer's eye away from the falcon and the pintail to the base."

For *Eternal Conflict*, Martin wanted a figure-eight design—a hawk sitting in two intertwining branches with a rattlesnake in its talons. "I initially drew the snake's head hanging down like a pendulum. The piece had a gothic-archway look with the head

in the bottom center. My wife thought that it looked boring, so I opened the rattlesnake's mouth, put in fangs, and turned the head. In the finished piece the snake and the bird are screaming at each other. I'm really happy with it."

Martin says that when working up an image, he tries to keep the details of sculpting out of his mind. Instead he concentrates only on the scene. "I may recall a vision of the bird in a particular stance, and then, based on my understanding of anatomy, recreate that vision within the confines of the wood."

In *Solemn Moment*, a falcon preys on a purple martin. "I hope the viewer uses his imagination to visualize the aerial display that led to the capture, and I also hope the viewer sees the reverence the falcon shows for its prey."

Solemn Moment is carved from West Indian mahogany.

Martin has used cherry wood for a number of projects. Some, like this hummingbird feeding from a trumpet flower, are remarkably dainty.

"The design began as three little lines drawn while I was doodling. I was trying to get lines that look nice together."

The flower and stem are carved from one piece of cherry. The piece stands eighteen inches high.

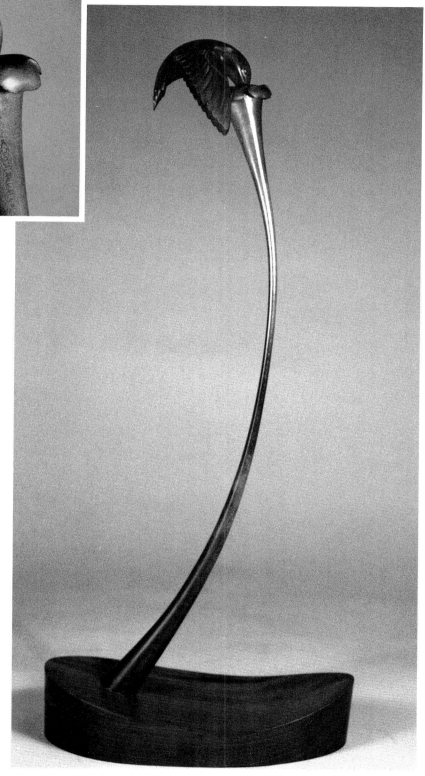

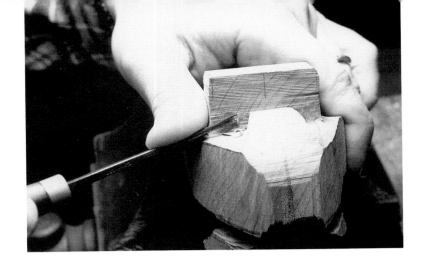

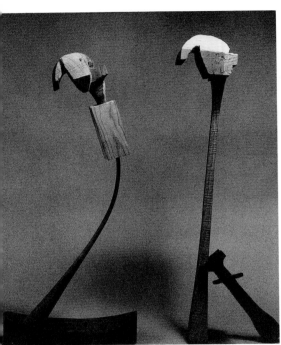

The bird feeds from a flower at the top of a long stem that curves and tapers to a quarter-inch diameter. To achieve the curve, Martin soaked the wood, which had been cut close to its final size, in hot tap water and then heated it with a propane torch.

"I put the piece in a vise and bent the wood gently so I could feel it give. Traditionally, wood has been heated with steam, bent, and then put into a form to hold it until the wood dries. But I felt that clamping might have broken the wood. Cherry is not very pliable and you have to be patient with it."

Working on small birds, Martin uses very small gouges. "I prefer to make a lot of tiny shavings. This takes the pressure off the wood and reduces the risk of breaking the piece."

This small preening sandpiper was done in 1987. Made from a single piece of walnut and mounted on a dowel, the bird reflects the style made famous by Elmer Crowell, a well-known Cape Cod decoy carver. Martin saw a

picture of one of Crowell's shorebirds positioned with one wing out and the head preening the underwing feathers, and he wanted to create his own.

For *Wetland Embrace*, done in 1986, Martin chose walnut because its color is perfect for the blackbird. "Originally I envisioned a composition of two birds, one lower than the other, but I felt the lower bird ruined the design, so I cut it away."

A blackbird and cattails make for a natural combination of bird and habitat. To make the cattails, he wet them with cold water, heated them with a blowtorch, and bent the stalks.

Martin is fond of doing shorebirds. "I enjoy sculpting birds that are on the land or in the water. I particularly like sculpting wading birds because I can experiment with the many different positions they make with their long legs and necks." Martin carved a walnut sandpiper in 1978 and a walnut avocet in 1985. The head and legs are separate pieces.

"I am intrigued with birds, especially birds in flight. I'd like to do a pair of scissor-tailed flycatchers in an aerial position.

"Another piece I have in mind for the future is a large white heron with plumage like a wedding veil that hangs back and can help hold up the bird."

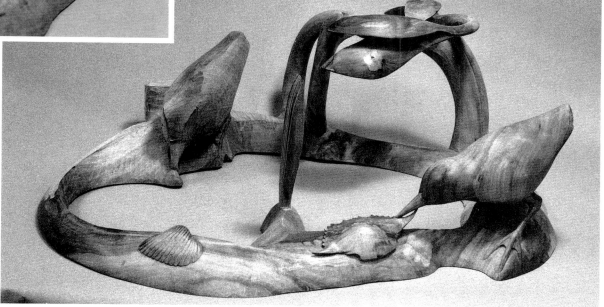

using apple wood, Martin wanted to do a piece that would incorporate five sandpipers. "I spent six or eight weeks on the sculpture without having a clear picture of the finished piece in my mind, a mistake I won't make again.

"By the time I set the piece aside, I'd carved in mangrove leaves, two sandpipers, and some beach habitat. The center of the piece was gone because I found rot in the apple log. The wood was beautiful, though. It had spalting that gave the effect of water splashing over sand."

Very large flocks of these Carolina parakeets used to live in the southeastern United States. Native to North America, the birds measured twelve inches long and inhabited gardens, farmlands, and suburban areas. The last ones seen in the wild were spotted in southern Florida in the 1920s.

Martin put branches and an apple in the composition. "One of the reasons these birds were killed was that they flew into orchards and destroyed the fruit. Hundreds of birds in a flock would descend upon an orchard and tear apart the apples just for the seeds. The birds were a close-knit group. The live ones would come back to the ones killed and they too would be shot."

One January day in 1989, Martin brought home a large pecan log that had been lying on the ground in his neighborhood for five or six years. He used a piece of the log for *A Flying Osprey*.

Ospreys measure twenty-one to twenty-five inches long and have a prominent wingspan often six feet in length. The log was heavy, weighing about five hundred pounds, and wide enough for Martin to carve the bird with its wings upright. After two weeks of chain sawing, Martin had the piece down to two hundred pounds. When finished, the composition weighed less than fifty pounds.

Snowy Essence features a snowy egret among lily pads, cattails, marsh plants, a frog, and even an alligator.

Of the frog and alligator, Martin says, "I enjoy doing them and they add to the story of the whole composition. It's fun to make them, but I won't carve a frog or alligator by itself and add it haphazardly. It must be unified with the rest of the sculpture."

"The most challenging part of the piece was removing the wood between the cattail leaves and head and then binding them."

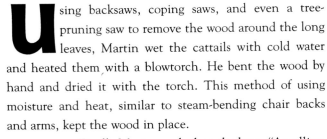

using backsaws, coping saws, and even a tree-pruning saw to remove the wood around the long leaves, Martin wet the cattails with cold water and heated them with a blowtorch. He bent the wood by hand and dried it with the torch. This method of using moisture and heat, similar to steam-bending chair backs and arms, kept the wood in place.

Finally Martin worked on the base. "An alligator, partially exposed, moving through water, adds danger and excitement. Having three characters, instead of just the egret and frog, completes the composition."

Martin likes the repeating curves on the egret's body and the cattail leaves and the reversing curves of the body, neck, and head. He also likes the negative and positive spaces he created between the legs of the egret, between the cattails, and between the bird and lily pads below it. "By drawing out the pattern carefully on paper, I can better visualize the carving and alter the negative and positive spaces if necessary."

Martin had seen a nature film of an osprey pulling a trout out of the water. The film, done in slow motion, gave him the idea to sculpt the event. "I thought the fish should be quite large, as large as a full-grown osprey can pull out of the water—a real test of the bird's capabilities."

Martin likes the light color of the wood. It is close to maple, with black lines of spalting that add interest. Spalting is caused by water and decay and the black lines are a fungus. Some day he wants to sculpt holly, a wood that is almost pure white and ideal for sculpture. But holly rarely grows more than two feet in diameter, and most hollies are half that size.

Martin designed this life-sized great blue heron with its delicate legs intact. What keeps the bird from breaking at the legs are the palm leaves. There are five points of contact between the leaves and the body, yet the entire composition is so delicate, the bird can actually be flexed or moved slightly. "When I suspend a piece, I use at least three points of contact to ensure stability, unless there's one spot that really ties the bird to the base with a lot of bulk. The points of contact are very small with no major intersections of body and leaf. I was concerned that the leaves would make the piece look too busy, but it maintains a natural look."

The bird's one straight leg is only a half inch in diameter at one point, while the other leg bends at the joint. "There is no strength there at all, which is a reason for the supporting leaves."

The composition has a great number of curves and reversing curves, and Martin added a luna moth for additional interest.

It took a year and a half for Martin to decide how he wanted to use a large piece of walnut. He knew he wanted to do a large bird or birds to take advantage of the crotch and fiddleback grain. After reading an article about how the Exxon *Valdez* oil spill was affecting nesting bald eagles, he decided: an eagle near an oil spill.

"I needed to express my feelings about how rotten we treat the world and all its creatures. I wanted the female eagle to be crying in pain and sorrow for what we've done to the world—ours and hers. I put a skull in the composition to shock people into realizing that each time we damage our world, we're killing ourselves."

Except for the head and feet, Martin kept the details of the eagle to a minimum. Large, polished surfaces on the body show off the walnut grain. To effect the look of oil on a beach, Martin used a propane torch to burn the base and halfway up the skull.

COURTESY MARTIN GATES

Eternal Conflict symbolizes the struggle between good and evil.

The center of the sculpture is open because the center of the cherry log was rotten. "Termites crawled out of the wood onto my arms, and I had to have the wood gassed at the pest control center." Streaks of maroon add to the beauty and design of the piece.

Martin originally planned to use the log for a pair of scissor-tailed flycatchers, but the worm holes would have spoiled that composition. "The wood was more appropriate for a masculine subject than a pair of dainty, graceful birds."

The feathers were done with a chip-carving knife and a one-quarter-inch mortising chisel. "I grouped the smaller feathers on the head into interesting shapes to give more expression."

The piece was done in 1988.

"I opened the rattlesnake's
mouth and put in the fangs.
The snake and the bird are
screaming at each other."

Martin chose to do
the composition in
West Indian mahogany
because he felt the color
enhanced the look of the
parakeet and habitat.

"The design began as
three little lines drawn as
I was doodling."

This avocet is a more stylized piece. Martin carved fewer feather groups and less detail. He wanted to show shapes rather than distinct feathers.

In *Solemn Moment* a falcon preys on a purple martin. The falcon, with a slight upward glance, observes a symbolic moment of silence before he begins his meal. "I purposely left the eyes off the face of the martin. I wanted the piece to say, 'This is nature. It's nothing personal, just survival.'"

Redhead Sleeper is Martin's version of a traditional sleeping decoy. To make the design his own and to add interest, he placed the bill on top of the wing.

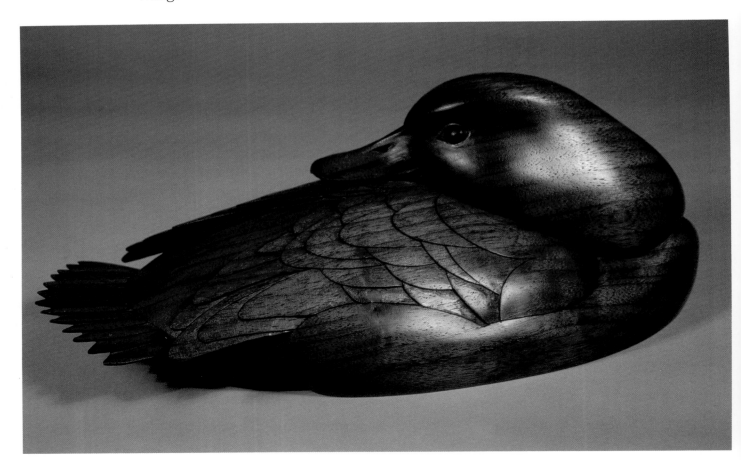

This walnut sandpiper is one of Martin's early shorebirds. It is done in a very traditional decoy style with carved feathers.

As a child Martin remembers seeing his uncle return from hunting trips with pheasants. These were his first encounters with the bird, and he thought they were beautiful.

Ring-necked pheasants had been successfully introduced in the United States in the 1880s outside of Lebanon, Oregon, Martin's hometown. There were still populations of the birds in that area when Martin was growing up, but farmers had not left trees to surround the fields or provide fence rows, and the pheasants literally had no place to run.

"I saw two pheasants taking flight, and I wanted to capture them a wing beat or two off the ground." Martin chose a large, forked-shaped piece of crotch mahogany for this composition, *Nowhere to Run*.

Grant Goltz

Theories Of Design

Grant Goltz of Hackensack, Minnesota, started carving hunting decoys when he was fifteen. "I was familiar with wood because my grandfather had a woodworking shop. I liked to draw, paint, and study birds. I was doing bird taxidermy and putting the birds into poses. If there was one thing that bought everything together for me, it was bird carving."

In 1973 he tried carving a decorative. "I had gone into a small woodcarving shop and had seen an array of carved birds, all crudely painted and stuck on driftwood. I told friends that the birds were bad because I couldn't figure out their species. My friends said that if I thought the carving was so bad, I should do better. I went home, carved a saw-whet owl, mounted it on wire legs and a piece of driftwood. I showed it to my friends and they encouraged me to carve more birds and to start selling them." Grant did a series of songbirds and small loons. They sold and he continued doing miniature songbirds. "I was not aware that carvers were doing full-sized birds. A year later I bought Bruce Burk's *Game Bird Carving* and saw for the first time what serious carvers were doing."

In 1975 Grant entered the International Decoy Contest in Davenport, Iowa, with two decorative waterfowl and two painted but untextured decoys. "I went with my boxes under my arms, walked into the tent, took one look around, and wanted to find a way to sneak out. The birds were fancy and nicely textured, but it was too late to leave, so I entered the amateur category. My scaup took honorable mention; my goldeneye won first place. Overall I got Best-in-Show with a blue-winged teal, while my wood duck took second in class behind the teal. I was hooked."

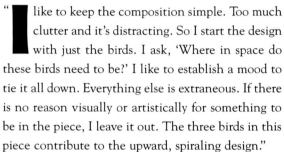

"I like to keep the composition simple. Too much clutter and it's distracting. So I start the design with just the birds. I ask, 'Where in space do these birds need to be?' I like to establish a mood to tie it all down. Everything else is extraneous. If there is no reason visually or artistically for something to be in the piece, I leave it out. The three birds in this piece contribute to the upward, spiraling design."

"I like to develop a flow in a piece that starts out low and brings the eye up, like a spiraling, curving line."

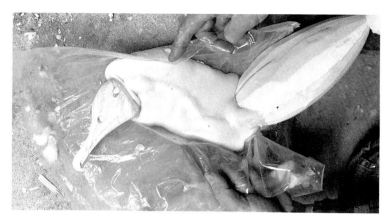

BLACK-AND-WHITE PHOTOGRAPHS ON PAGES 91 TO 98,
100 TO 103, AND 110 BY GRANT GOLTZ

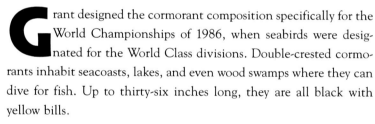

Grant designed the cormorant composition specifically for the World Championships of 1986, when seabirds were designated for the World Class divisions. Double-crested cormorants inhabit seacoasts, lakes, and even wood swamps where they can dive for fish. Up to thirty-six inches long, they are all black with yellow bills.

Grant decided to carve cormorants as a tribute to a friend of his, a Minnesota gunner who hunted ducks on Gull Lake, in central Minnesota. He knew that on days when the ducks avoided the lake, the gunner would shoot the resident cormorants.

Grant began the cormorant composition by making Styrofoam models. With a Styrofoam body cut to size, Grant poured a two-part foam for the neck. He confined the foam with plastic as it expanded to the form of the neck. Then he attached the carved foam tail and added more to build up the back of the body.

Grant used an air-filled drum sander to shape
the foam body and did the final shaping with
a Surfoam rasp. He cut the neck to make some
adjustments and then rejoined the pieces.

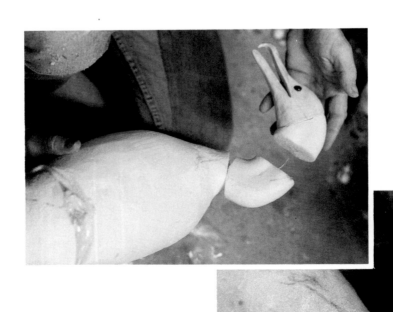

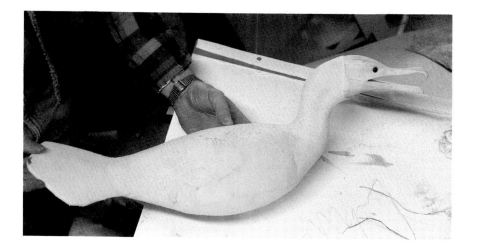

Knowing that the World Championships' rules required more than one bird, Grant felt that any even number would make for an uninteresting design. "I figured that three birds would give a spiraling motion to the piece, but I didn't want all three birds to look alike. So I included one immature bird, which is the lowest."

To get some height to the piece and to create an irregular, asymmetrical design, Grant positioned one bird on a low rock. The next bird is higher up with its wings draped out to dry. Those wings, along with the head and neck of the bird, lead the eye to the third and uppermost bird, completing the circular design.

Three birds give a spiraling motion to the piece.

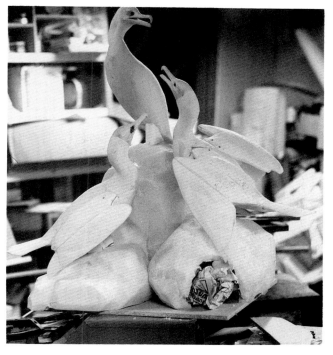

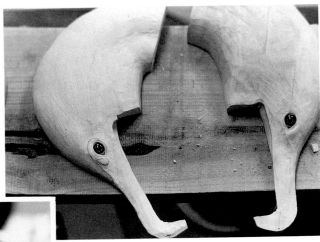

Grant hollows all his bird bodies, including the heads, because he likes to reduce internal stress and prefers to place his glass eyes on the insides of the heads to avoid using wood fillers. He shapes both the inside and outside of the eye openings. For one cormorant he makes a separate lower mandible. Another has its bill closed, and the mandible is defined with a burning pen. Grant uses a burning pen at the feather intersections to raise the head feathers slightly. He gives these feathers more definition by using a small grinding stone and a burning pen.

"I like their snakey heads and their reptilian look."

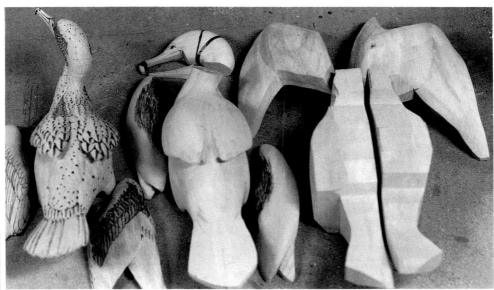

To facilitate hollowing a body, Grant uses two pieces of wood, hollows each, and then glues the halves together. He also makes the wings separately.

He clamps the head and body halves together with rubber bands made from pieces of inner tubes.

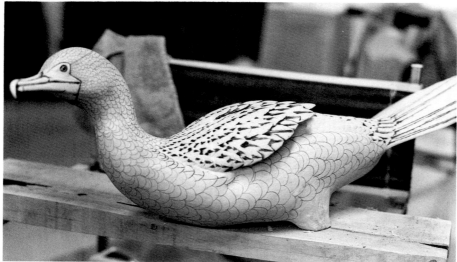

Grant fits a partially completed wing onto the body to check the layout of the scapular feathers. Using small ruby carvers and a flat, pointed burning tip, he details the scapulars and the shafts on the larger feathers. Grant treats the underside feathers on each cormorant differently. The juvenile has narrow and slightly ragged-looking feathers. The adult's feather tips are more even. The wet adult bird's feathers are bunched and rougher.

rant decided on three yellow-headed blackbirds for the 1987 World Championships. Songbirds were designated for that year's world-class entries. Working with Styrofoam, he made models and then used sticks to hold the models aloft while he experimented with positions. He decided to mount the birds on phragmites. The piece is titled *Sun Kings*.

"I knew I wanted a composition of three birds, and I had a fairly clear idea of how I'd position the birds and how they would relate to each other."

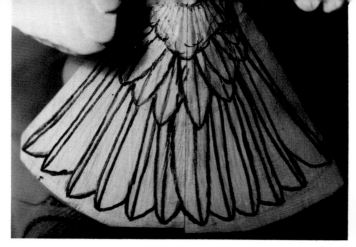

rant works on laying out the tail feathers and uses a ruby carver to define them. Next he begins to make the ruffled feathers on the body.

L aying out the feathers, Grant works the topside first and finishes it even before he removes wood from the underside. Most songbirds have only nine visible primaries. The feather layout completed, he defines the wing feathers and separations with a ruby carver and sands the wing.

"I did not see a free-form base as part of the original composition. I feel that a formal base is an unnecessary component, but with this piece, the dense concentration of sedge leaves at the bottom of the finished piece could not visually balance the birds, so I added a black, lacquered base."

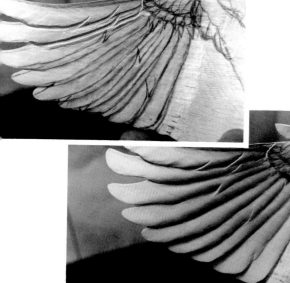

Grant says that the weight of the birds was a challenge. To deal with it, he hollowed the blackbirds' bodies. In some places the wood is only a sixteenth of an inch thick, and the top bird became so light that it weighs less than one ounce. "I experimented a little and found that the metal stem could support about three ounces before bending down to the angle I wanted. I cut the birds into halves and hollowed each. Some of the spaces between the ruffled feathers on the heads and necks actually go all the way through to the hollow centers of the birds. Even the bases of the wings of the upper bird are hollowed."

To fluff up this blackbird, Grant first carves the upper mandible and the feathered part of the throat from the main block of wood. These are shaped and ready to receive the lower mandible, which is carved separately to permit detail work on the mouth and throat. The lower mandible is then installed, and the head, textured and burned, is ready to seal and paint.

"Wood never dies. It's always moving and changing. When I design these carvings, I want them to be long-lasting. I don't know what environmental changes these carvings will be subjected to. They may end up in the Southwest desert or they may be exposed to repeated cycles of shrinking and expanding, so I remove wood from the inside of these carvings to reduce the chances for problems."

To hollow a bird, Grant makes the body and head separately. He splits them in half and hollows them as much as he can.

He does not like to use wood filler, so he strives for perfect glue joints. To do this, he attaches a piece of sandpaper to a milled-steel table top, puts pencil marks on the wood edges, and pulls the pieces in one direction until the pencil lines disappear.

"To glue the halves together, I use rubber bands that I make from inner tubes. I encase the bird like a mummy. It's like wrapping an Ace bandage around a limb. The pressure is tremendous. When the glue dries, I sand the joint so that it can't be seen."

Hollowing the wood reduces stress that might otherwise cause the wood halves to separate. "Wood, as it expands and contracts, pushes against itself in the middle and will push open at the edges. But there isn't any middle with my pieces. I have a shell with no stress.

"I hollow everything, sometimes to the point that if you were to put a light inside, you would see the glow."

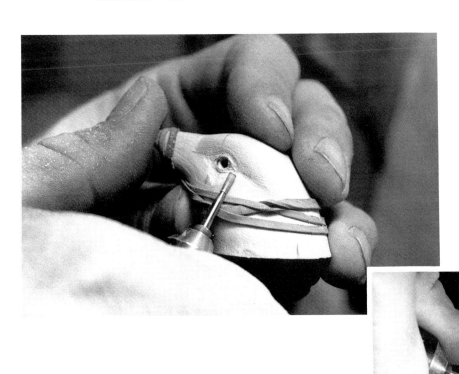

Grant hollows not only the bodies but also the heads. He cuts both body and head vertically along the back and top of the head. Later he disguises the glue with feather texturing. Grant will not use wood filler on his birds. Wood shrinks and expands, but the wood filler doesn't, so separations, even hairline in size, will eventually occur. Carvers often use fillers with glass eyes. To form an eyelid or close a gap, Grant must set the eyes from inside the head.

Once the head is hollowed, Grant carves a finished eye opening inside the head. He uses ruby carvers and thins the opening around the eye to the thickness of the bird's eyelid. "The shape of the inside of the eye socket should be the same shape as the surface of the glass eye. Before the final fitting, I must keep in mind not only the profile shape of the opening but also the three-dimensional curve from top to bottom and side to side. That's the only difficult part."

Grant temporarily sets the glass eyes into the openings with sculpting wax. Once he has them positioned correctly, he uses epoxy to glue them in place, and then he removes the wax.

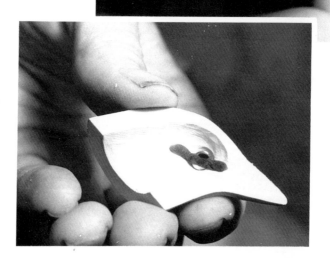

Grant uses oversized eyes, because they allow him to create eye corners, which are common not only to humans but also to birds.

hen Grant decided to make an owl, he carved a facial mask as a separate piece, put the eyes into the back of it, and glued the mask to the head. "One disadvantage with this technique is that I have only one chance to get the expression right. So I check that the eyes are looking in the same direction and sticking out equally on both sides. Birds don't move their eyes around much, and it's important to get the right facial expression.

"People ask me how many heads I throw away. I've never done one that came out wrong. It's not very complicated. I've taught this technique to beginning duck carvers, and they all were able to do it."

Sora rails are common in Minnesota, so when Grant planned to do a composition of three sora rails on lily pads, he went to the marshes and wild rice beds to collect a dozen birds for reference. To make a realistic model of the composition, he made three taxidermy models and used Styrofoam for the three lily pads and stems. The uppermost bird is landing, the middle rail has both feet on the pad, and the lowest has one foot on the pad and one off.

Wild rice stems support the flying bird. The stems will be supported by a stylized turtle shell. The setting for this piece is northern Minnesota's wild rice country, also the home of the Ojibwa people. "Since the Ojibwas call Minnesota 'turtle shell,' I feel the turtle shell makes an appropriate base."

The lily pads are made of walnut. Grant found an unseasoned walnut log, flattened one end, and sketched the outlines of the pads on the surface. He planned the design so that the center of the log would not be part of the pads, because the wood had not dried out. "If you're going to put strain and stress on a drying log, you have to open the middle so the wood has a place to go when it shrinks." The opening between the two pads is at the center of the log. The entire base, including the stems, was carved from the walnut log. "The stems look frail and fragile, but I didn't need a lot of mass to balance things out. It's a pretty compact piece, yet the base is light and airy."

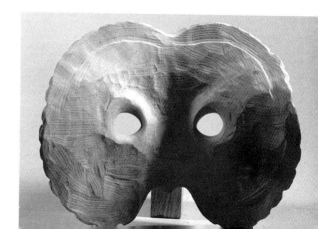

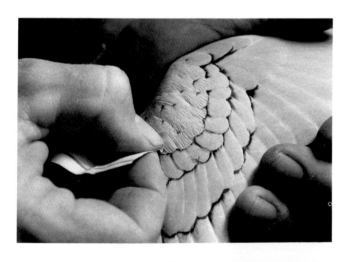

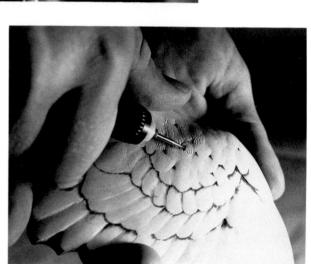

The spread wings of the landing sora rail are made from single pieces of wood. Grant doesn't use inserts because he feels they create a shingled look and he likes a look in which the feathers are defined and separate but still blended together. To raise the feathers, Grant uses a diamond bit or sometimes works a spatula-shaped burning tip into corners and even under the wood. He cleans up the intersections with a pointed shading tip. If he wants feathers raised even more, he will grind out more wood with a diamond bit.

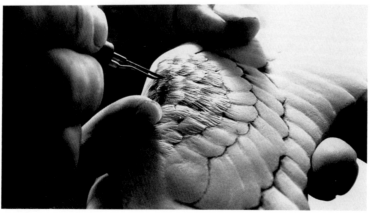

For reference Grant has an aviary and an indoor pond. Made of glass concrete, the pond measures seven feet in diameter. He views the ducks through a half-inch-thick piece of plate glass that is two and a half feet wide by five feet high. The pond is filled three feet deep with water, and the glass extends about a foot and a half below the water's surface.

Grant can observe at eye level ducks swimming with views above the water and below. "I can get an undistorted view of the whole body, even the feet and legs. When the lights are off, the birds really don't see me, so I can study feathers and even see how the body pulsates and breathes."

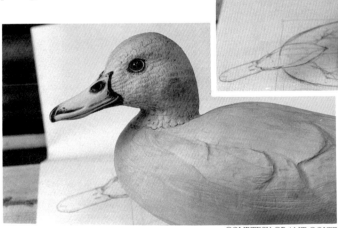

COURTESY GRANT GOLTZ

COURTESY GRANT GOLTZ

rant has also built a platform above the pond to allow him a top view. "The real shape from above isn't quite what you anticipate. Many diving ducks are amazingly square on the front end. The widest point is back where the legs are. I don't see many divers carved that way. I see fat, teardrop-shaped birds."

"I wanted a scene representative of northern Minnesota, so I went to a swamp and found samples of the phragmites and sedge leaves. I decided to place the leaves at the bottom of the composition because I needed a visual mass to offset the heavy look of the birds." Grant used hot-melt glue to work out an arrangement of phragmites and sedge leaves and decided to use two stems of phragmites to support the three birds. "I did the arranging in about two hours and put it aside for two days. Then I added some components and that was it. It came together fast."

COURTESY GRANT GOLTZ

The yellow-breasted blackbird is an appealing combination of colors: mostly black with bright yellow on the head and upper breast. Native Americans in southern Minnesota and farther south in the Mississippi Valley used the yellow feathers from the heads and necks of these birds to make robes for their chiefs. The sun was important to these agricultural peoples, so it was fitting that a ruler wear a robe as bright as the sun. Grant titled his composition *Sun Kings.*

"I designed the piece around three points of color to build in strength as the eye moves up the piece. I wanted visual motion with the colors. The female, a subdued yellow, is the lowest, and the most dramatic bird is at the top."

Color is important. Black lets the yellow in the feathers stand out, which in turn complements the color of the phragmites.

"The phragmite stems contribute to the visual motion because they give the illusion of being blown in the wind. I gave the middle bird ruffled feathers to add to the effect of a windy day. Even the motion of the brass stems, which pick up the slightest vibration, adds to the effect. After I constructed the vegetation, I almost didn't want to carve the birds. The stems were brass and the piece looked like a beautiful metal sculpture. It seemed a crime to stick birds on it."

The stems were constructed from solid brass rods to hold the weight of the birds. Even so the stem that holds the two birds bends more than six to eight inches when the birds are placed on it.

To make the fluffy parts of the phragmites, Grant took dental floss and stretched pieces between two nails on a board. On the dental floss he placed drops of yellow carpenter's glue and pinches of plaster of Paris. He rolled the mix between his fingers to achieve the look of seed heads. By leaving extra floss at either end, he had both a stem and a length that he frayed out. Afterward, he sprayed these pieces with lacquer.

"This is a spring courtship composition. Seed heads in the spring look ragged. In the fall, they have three times as much fluff and seed, but by that time three quarters of the seeds have fallen off from the effects of wind and rain."

Because Grant included an immature bird in the composition, he decided to add two adult birds in summer plumage rather than in spring breeding plumage. "One thing that bothers me is birds in plumage that are inappropriate. How often have you seen a fall hunting scene featuring a fully plumed drake blue-winged teal?"

Grant wanted three birds in *On Bill's Rock Pile*, and he didn't want all three to look alike.

Bill, for whom the piece is named, is the market gunner who inspired the piece. He died two weeks before the piece was exhibited at the World Championships.

rant made two sightings of the great gray owl, the largest owl in North America. The first was in January 1980. Grant saw the owl perched on the dead branch of a balsam tree at the edge of a pine plantation in a remote area of northern Minnesota. "I waded through the snow until I was directly beneath it. The facial disk was spectacular, and it just looked at me with its yellow eyes. I knew then that I wanted to carve this bird. It was inside me wanting to get out."

The great gray owl is the most heavily feathered bird in North America. The bird can puff itself up to look enormous, though internally the body is small. A specimen Grant measured was twenty-nine inches long, but half of that length was tail feathers.

To give height to the composition, which measures four feet high, Grant put the bird in a tall branch that sits on a weathered piece of wood.

The vole is common prey for the great gray owl. Grant trapped a vole and placed it exactly as it would hang from the owl's beak.

The great gray owl is also called the ghost owl, and the swamp where Grant spotted his second great gray is called Drumbeater Bog. He titled the piece *Gray Ghost of Drumbeater Bog*.

"This was my first piece that did not have a furniture-style base with a routed edge."

"This is a typical spring courtship scene I've often observed. I carved these ruddy ducks for the World Pairs. I wanted to present the birds in a composition rather than as separate birds in a tank. Both the poses of the individual ducks and their relationship to each other are important. The small arrangement of weathered bulrushes emphasizes the relationship and allows the composition to float as a unit."

"The hardest part of this piece was engineering and balancing it to float properly. The piece had to be meticulously weighted, and I had to fashion some of the bulrushes out of solid lead."

"On the study bird I noticed the scapular feather had a soft, bluish iridescence. At a different angle it looked green, and at yet another angle it turned dark. I used Interference colors to capture this variety."

To paint the cinnamon teal's iridescent colors, Grant experimented with Interference colors made by Golden Matte Acrylics. Though all jars of these colors look white, they do show color if held to a light source at a certain angle. They change from color to its complement. A blue will change to an orange and a violet will change to a yellow, depending on the angle of the light.

"I wanted the birds to be swimming and moving, not just sitting there. I wanted the female to stand out in the composition, so I positioned her closest to the viewer. The male's bright colors form the backdrop for the female's soft subtleties."

"**A**t the time this carving was made, it was difficult to get realistic-looking, colored glass eyes for the drake cinnamon teal. So I had eyes specially made by Tohickon. I also had trouble weighting the piece to float correctly."

Jim Hazeley

Vignetting

He has been interested in design since he was a child, Jim Hazeley says, and today he designs floors, ceilings, and furniture for Armstrong Corporation. "I have always considered myself an applied artist, which means I apply aesthetics to commercial products."

When did Jim turn his artistic talents to bird carving? In 1974 he attended the Lancaster County Woodcarvers Show and saw Ernest Muehlmatt's carvings. He liked them so much that he bought a pair. Jim went to other bird carving shows, found a copy of Bruce Burk's *Game Bird Carving*, carved a green-winged teal, and entered it in a local show. "I put an outrageous price on the piece and it sold. That was encouraging."

Eventually he discovered the World Championships. In 1983 he entered several birds as a novice and took Best-in-Category in both seabirds and birds of prey, as well as two seconds and a third for songbirds, waterfowl, and game birds. His barn owl won Best-in-Show. "I realized that this is what I'm about. Bird carving is totally fulfilling, and I am very fortunate to know that. Very few people can find that one thing they can do better than anything else."

Jim carves a variety of birds, from raptors to shorebirds to songbirds, and he is particularly interested in new ways of designing. "If we bird carvers are going to call ourselves fine artists, we must experiment. We can't get stuck in a rut doing realistic birds and elaborate habitats." Jim's compositions bring together realistic and natural wood techniques in novel ways. He calls his approach vignetting.

"I had to do this bird to
get it out of my system."

J im began to think about doing a saw-whet owl after he visited a raptor center in Virginia Beach, Virginia. He relied heavily on personal observations of saw-whets and on references, such as television programs and videotapes. "What does it take to be able to do a bird well? You need a real sense of what a bird is like as a living creature, preferably by seeing it first-hand in the wild or in a zoo. But you can also achieve this with film footage if it is sufficiently comprehensive."

Jim saw a photograph of a saw-whet owl squatting down on a branch with its head tilted up and its lower eyelid starting to close. "That pose was part of this image that was in my mind. The pose is just as important as the carving of a particular species."

From the films Jim studied, he had the impression that saw-whets are fierce little owls. "They'll prey on mice and small birds, and some of their prey are almost as big as they are. They'll sometimes kill as many as seven or eight birds in a night, eating only the heads." But Jim did not want a dead bird in his composition, so instead he decided on a butterfly.

"A saw-whet owl will feed on insects, though they are not the owl's favorite prey. I wanted the butterfly's colors to contribute to the composition without distracting the viewer from the owl." He chose a falcate orangetip, with its white body and orange wingtips.

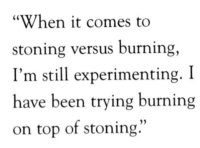

"When it comes to stoning versus burning, I'm still experimenting. I have been trying burning on top of stoning."

Jim uses a variety of stones to achieve the different effects of texture on the owl. Using a sharp stone and burning deeply, he achieves a hairy look. With a pointed stone, he can get sharp but shallow little undercuts. "When it comes to stoning versus burning, I'm still experimenting, trying to find the optimum combination. I have been trying burning on top of stoning. Stoning has a softer, less-precise look, and I think stoning is more effective on breasts and bellies. I like fine-burning the primaries." For deep undercuts, he uses a long, narrow burning tip.

The body of the falcate orangetip is one inch long and made of tupelo. To replicate the soft surface textures, Jim glued sawdust to the back end and ground-up foam rubber to the thorax area. "The back end is soft and not really furry, but the thorax is." The foam rubber, which he bought at a model train store where it is sold as simulated grass, gives a fuzzy effect, and it can be glued down and painted. "Most any other material tends to mat down. Foam rubber is not organic, so it doesn't break down and mat. Instead, it stays springy." Once it was glued down and hardened with Super Glue, Jim was able to paint the material easily.

Jim uses two-part Duro modeling putty to shape legs, toes, pads, and even eyerings and eyelids. It comes in a flat, ribbon form, half blue and half yellow. Cutting off a piece, he kneads it until it is uniformly green. Then it can be worked like clay. "I have about an hour and a half working time before it begins to stiffen. Other epoxies are too grainy or sticky.

"Because the Duro does not harden quickly, it can be worked for a while with a variety of tools, such as dental picks. To keep a tool from sticking to the epoxy, I keep some modeling clay handy and touch the tool to the clay. The oil in the clay keeps the epoxy from sticking."

What may be Jim's most dramatic piece is a pair of airborne miniature eagles that he carved in 1985. Mating behavior brings these birds together in the air. Locking talons, they will tumble for hundreds of feet then disengage and soar back up for a repeat performance. It's an aerial ballet that may start thousands of feet up.

As a courtship ritual prior to nesting, a mated pair will fly high, as if in a mock battle, to perform an aerial ballet.

"My challenge with the piece was getting the eagles convincingly suspended above the base. I watched a television show set in the Rockies and saw some gnarly, windswept black spruce trees, and I thought I could make one to support the birds. One eagle's outstretched wing touches the tree, and the birds are joined together." The piece is titled *Mating Flight*.

Jim also does pairs of birds in simple, standing poses, such as these two miniature male prairie chickens. The composition shows typical mating behavior. One male, his head down, air sacs inflated, and in a characteristic courtship dance pose, has invaded the territory of the other bird, which has its head up. The fanned tail, the drooping wings, the erect ear tufts, and inflated air sacs are all part of the courtship dance used to attract the attention of the female.

"**A** piece I describe as environmental is the purple gallinule on a lily pad. Twelve to fourteen inches long, this green and blue bird inhabits freshwater marshes and ponds. This composition is a typical slice of life for this bird. I couldn't imagine carving the gallinule without putting it on a lily pad. It has those huge feet and long toes that enable it to walk on top of the lily pads in search of snails and small crustaceans on the undersides of the pads." The life-sized gallinule, in a typical hunting pose, was done in 1985.

rouching down with its beak pointing out like a rapier, the green heron feeds on fish, crustaceans, and insects in rivers, marshes, and moist woodlands. Up to twenty-two inches long, the green heron has a greenish back and a purplish belly.

When Jim designed the piece, he thought he would have the bird standing on a root that was coming out of the water, but he changed his mind and decided to have a rock rising out of water. On the water he carved lily pads. Working with a piece of walnut three inches thick, he carved the base of the rock in the walnut, and from that emerges a piece of detailed tupelo.

The heron assumes this poised-arrow hunting pose at the edge of a stream or pond, waiting for a fish to come by. Jim says the composition is daggerlike.

Jim created the heron in 1989 for the North American Shorebird Championship sponsored by the Wetlands Institute of Stone Harbor, New Jersey. The piece took Best-in-Show.

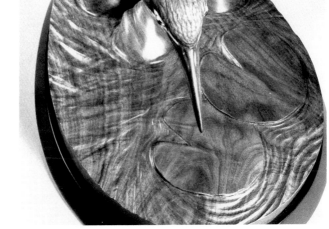

"I saw this bird hunting in a salt marsh near Cape May, New Jersey. The bird sat patiently in this position for a long time."

Jim created this Cooper's hawk for the 1989 World Championship miniature division. This bird measures fifteen to twenty inches long and is similar to a sharp-shinned hawk, only larger. With a dark blue back and white and rusty bars on its chest and under its wings, the Cooper's hawk lives in forests and preys on small mammals and birds. The prey in this piece is a brown-headed cowbird.

"I pictured most of the composition in my mind before I started carving. I saw the piece shaped as an isosceles triangle with the Cooper's hawk at the apex."

Jim has recently done a number of life-sized hummingbird compositions. One piece has a ruby-throated hummingbird feeding on honeysuckle that entwines barbed wire. The habitat was fabricated from wood, copper sheets, and copper and aluminum wire. Another piece has a hooklike composition with the bird feeding from a cardinal flower. The stem is made from tupelo with wire in it.

"Inexperienced carvers are paying more attention to carving than to the bird underneath its feathers. I like to see artists take carefully studied anatomical liberties with their work in order to improve the artistic qualities of their carvings. I've tried that with some of my flying birds to give them artistic curves."

All of Jim's birds are detachable from the base or the environment. A couple of his early pieces with fixed attachments cracked with the shock of transport, so Jim now designs his compositions so the birds can be detached. He keeps a supply of round and square brass tubing from one-sixteenth inch to one-quarter inch to connect a bird like the bobwhite quail to its mounting point. Each size of tubing telescopes neatly into the next larger size, enabling Jim to remove the bird from its habitat. He has devised a metal-to-metal connection using two telescoping sizes resulting in a pin on one part, usually the bird, and a socket into which the pin fits on the other part, usually the habitat.

When there are two points or more of contact, Jim uses a round pin, and when there is only one point of contact, a socket connection. The latter connection prevents the bird from rotating on its perch.

When two pins are used, they must be precisely parallel to each other from the point at which they come out of the bird or they will not slide in and out of their sockets. Keeping the connections parallel is a common problem when making two holes for two connections. Using Bondo, Jim drills the holes in the branch much larger than necessary and fills the gaps with Bondo. Then he sets the bird in place by slipping the tubes that would be the sockets in place over the pins on the bird's feet. To facilitate this technique, he usually applies a thin film of Vaseline to any part that might contact the Bondo and cause it to adhere.

"I like to have the bird doing something."

Easily recognized by its brilliant color, the scarlet tanager measures no more than seven and a half inches long and can be found in the eastern half of the United States. The composition is not elaborate. A branch of a hop flower tree curls around the bird in a pleasing sweep.

In a chickadee composition, the bird sits, head cocked, eyeballing a ladybug. "I hate pieces that don't seem to have any real reason for being. I like to have the bird doing something, and the ladybug gives the chickadee a reason for sitting on the branch."

When painting birds, Jim is aware of how the colors will look in different lighting conditions. He is particularly concerned with metamerism, the property of color that allows the changes of hues and values, depending on the nature of the light source. Before painting a bird, Jim is careful to learn under what conditions the piece is going to be viewed. Because most carvings are viewed in residential settings with incandescent, or warm, lighting, he usually paints under incandescent light.

GREG HEISEY

"I was inspired to do the blue grouse piece after I read an article on blue grouse that was accompanied by superb photography. I had previously done a miniature male sage grouse, and the article got me thinking it was time to do one of the great western grouse life-sized. I found I had access to good reference materials, so I did a mature male in full courtship display."

" I chose to do a screech owl, both because I wanted to and because I had very good reference material. Although I might want to carve a particular bird, if I do not have and can't feasibly get sufficient reference, I can't do the piece. Still photography alone, no matter how extensive, is never enough. If I have not observed the bird myself in the wild, I at least have to have seen it on film to get a sense of what the bird is like as a living creature, how it moves, and what it does or does not do. I also find that it is almost impossible to carve a bird without having access to a dead specimen, a skin, or a mount to acquire intimate details and dimensions that no photograph can provide. This is not the first owl I carved. This piece was commissioned after a client had seen my first."

"I chose to give this bird a mouse as its prey. I will almost never carve a bird of prey in a static pose. I posed this bird in a watchful attitude—it's looking out for mouse-stealers."

"I still feel that my perfect kestrel is yet to be achieved."

"**T**he kestrel is one of my favorite birds. Before I did this piece, I carved two others, neither of which, in hindsight, I felt was particularly well done. I was determined to carve one that I would be happy with. This is the best I have done so far, but I still feel that my perfect kestrel is yet to be achieved."

" I had carved a number of miniature eagles, but I had yet to try a life-sized piece. I came across some truly outstanding reference for the inside of the bill and throat of an eagle and got itching to at least carve a life-sized head.

"It so happened that I was carving this head at the time of the tragic plane crash that claimed the lives of so many of the 101st Airborne Division, the Screaming Eagles. The coincidence touched me, and I dedicated the piece to those who had died.

"For the mourning dove, I decided against a lot of foliage. I ended up with a simple environment." Working with a block of basswood, Jim carved a pebbly base for the dove.

"My favorite subjects tend to be birds of prey or game birds."

When Jim paints a piece, he most often uses a Langnickel no. 1 or no. 2. He warns against using too small a brush. A tiny brush gives too short a paint stroke. "People think that the smaller the brush, the finer the line, but that's not necessarily true."

"The most difficult part of the piece was the crest. Carvers used to stylize it or use inserts, and it would end up looking a bit like a fright wig."

Jim's painting strategy brings together light and dark tones. For instance, to paint a common brown feather, he might use Jo Sonja's smoked pearl for the light tones, and for the dark, earth colors, he might apply raw umber, raw sienna, and burnt umber, the last being the darkest color. Going back and forth with the brush, he blends lighter and darker tones, building depth that can be found on real feathers by building light and dark brush strokes on top of each other.

Pointing out that the quill area on many feathers will be dark with lighter edges, he puts down a base color about midway and starts at the quill with a dark color, pulling it out with the brush toward the edge using many fine brush strokes. Then, taking a light color, he works from the edge and pulls the color into the dark area. To the middle he applies a medium-tone color. "I do that three or four times, pulling lights into darks and vice versa and applying middle tones. All this achieves the visual depth of a real feather."

"A raptor with prey tells its own story. The fierce-looking hawk holds a brown-headed cowbird in its talons."

"I created this piece for the North American Songbird Championship sponsored by Ducks Unlimited. I wanted to use a flowering cactus in the environment, and I chose the rufous both because it is common to the Southwest and because I happen to consider it to be particularly handsome. I decided against suspending the bird with its bill stuck into the flower. I wanted instead to put a bird in flight so the piece would be different from every hummingbird-in-flight piece I had ever seen. The piece took Best-in-Show."

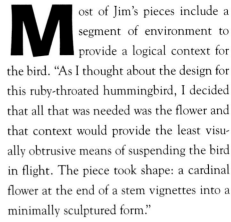

Most of Jim's pieces include a segment of environment to provide a logical context for the bird. "As I thought about the design for this ruby-throated hummingbird, I decided that all that was needed was the flower and that context would provide the least visually obtrusive means of suspending the bird in flight. The piece took shape: a cardinal flower at the end of a stem vignettes into a minimally sculptured form."

Jim did this piece for the Wetlands Institute in Stone Harbor, New Jersey. It was auctioned at their annual fund-raising festival.

"I believe I was one of the first to use a flat-finished paint called Jo Sonja, which I found while I was searching for a gouache appearance. A gouache works on paper because its pigment binds to the paper's porous fibers. But I haven't had much luck using gouache on a bird because first you have to seal the bird, and, once it's sealed, the gouache washes off because it has no film binder, no strength. That's why everyone paints with acrylics and oils. They form a strong film and adhere to a nonporous surface.

"I have painted with both acrylics and oils. A big drawback to oils is the need to hold the bird while painting it. Rapid-drying acrylics make this easy. I've also found acrylics have an inherent sheen that is sometimes okay, but often it's too high for the bird. And you can't tone it down without affecting the color. The only other potentially usable paints I know of are tempera and casein, but they're soluble and meant for porous canvas or paper.

"What Jo Sonja paints offer is a dead, flat look, which is usually what I'm after. I can make it shinier if that's the effect I want. Because Jo Sonja paints are not soluble when dry but not as tough as pure acrylics, I've learned to protect the paint with a flat, lacquer finish called Testors Dull Cote. Jo Sonja paints burnish, so I have to be careful when handling the bird."

"**J**o Sonja paints have a slightly better open time than acrylics since they take a little longer to dry. Acrylics have a fast drying time, and once dry they can never soften up again unless you apply alcohol or ketone solvents. Jo Sonja paints are even more insoluble than regular acrylics once they are dry, though they are more sensitive to abrasion."

Jim has since found other interesting properties of Jo Sonja paints. When he was working with acrylics, he could not use titanium white directly from a tube. He found it too stark, particularly since he mixes his paints to look warm. "I'm inclined to mix a color to the warm side. And for a cold color like a blue, I will usually subdue it a bit with a warm wash. For a white I mix titanium white with raw umber in proportions of ten or twenty to one. When I started experimenting with Jo Sonja paints, I discovered that smoked pearl is identical to a mix of white and raw umber."

"I created these two pieces for an entirely practical reason. I knew they would sell."

"The tree does more than just suggest a season; it also suspends the bird."

Inspired by a painting of a fox chasing a ruffed grouse, Jim decided to have a fox going after a pheasant. "This is an action-filled composition. The pheasant bursts up from the fox. The predator has lost its prey. The fox holds only a feather in its mouth. This is an environmental piece as well. The tree and snow on the base suggest an early spring day. But the tree does more than just suggest a season; it also suspends the bird. A brass branch comes under and touches a rear-wing feather."

"In 1988 a very good client of mine saw a blue jay I had carved and, being an admirer of blue jays, asked me to carve one in full flight. At first I didn't have a clear picture of what I wanted to carve, but finally I decided on a flying bird in a banking position. I wanted the point of contact to be nothing more than a wingtip brushing by a base. At first I intended to develop some habitat, but I couldn't think of anything that would enhance the vitality of the bird itself, and I knew I did not want to hang the bird in the air from an abstract form. I found a particularly interesting piece of wood and decided to keep the composition simple. I didn't want an environment. I'm perfectly pleased with the piece.

"I chose the pose to put as much dynamism into the bird as I could, showing him in a banked turn with feathers splayed to the max."

"I just wanted the bird brushing by the base. There was enough going on with just that."

"The upsweeping wings of the lower bird make contact with the underside of the downsweeping wings of the upper bird. The design gives a circular flow to the birds."

GREG HEISEY

"I wanted to do
a cerulean warbler
because they are
unique, they are
appealing, and I had
excellent reference
materials."

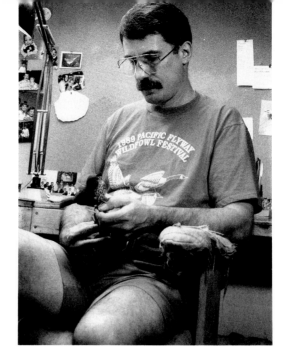

Peter Kaune

Capturing Essence

Growing up in a rural area in the state of Washington, Peter Kaune loved the outdoors and birds. He remembers making coot decoys out of papier-mâché and trying to decoy birds with them. Birds were his passion until he turned fifteen, when they were replaced by cars and sports. It took twenty years to get him back to birds. When he bought an English sports car and was restoring its wooden frame, he found he needed to do some carving. At about the same time, he noticed a magazine feature on bird carvers and decided to try combining his new interest in wood carving with his old interest in birds. His first fifty carvings were natural-finish shorebirds made out of oak and pine. They sold, and he began doing decorative decoys, selling them for $25. Two hundred decoys later he was getting $500 a bird.

In 1979 he picked up a copy of Bruce Burk's *Game Bird Carving* and copies of *North America Decoys* magazine. He attended his first carving show. A year later he entered two decoys, a mallard drake and a harlequin, in the Pacific Flyway Decoy Association Show. "The harlequin didn't float right and the oversized mallard took only a third in the novice class. But six months later I entered the California Open in San Diego with a decorative widgeon drake. It took Best-in-Show in the intermediate class. Once I got started on decorative birds, I got hooked on the detail. I just knew this was what I wanted to pursue."

Peter posed this three-inch-long robin to stand on a piece of carved and painted manzanita. "I wanted to do a single, miniature robin in a winter state. I've noticed that the bird will sit up in a tree for long periods of time, and I think I caught that with the carving. It's difficult to carve a bird fluffed up in the wintertime because it can end up looking fat instead of fluffy."

"I was originally going to do evening grosbeaks for the Worlds. I collected my materials and waited for the grosbeaks to arrive. I waited and waited, but they never came. The robins are here year-round, and I had plenty of opportunity to observe them. By the time the nomadic grosbeaks showed up, there was one week left until the competition."

Peter used clay models to help him visualize how the birds related to each other and to the branch they are perched on. Both the placement of the birds and their colors are factors in this composition.

For the competition, the robins could not exceed eight inches in length, so Peter had to do most of the carving under a magnifying glass. "If you work with magnification, it seems like you're working on a full-sized bird."

The branches of the composition cascade down an oblong black base. Peter wanted to create V shapes and spent hours adding and subtracting branches to get the right balance. He felt the placement of the birds was critical and ended up with one slightly lower than the other. One of the robins, the upper bird, has its beak open, while the other has a closed mouth.

The thrush was one of the first birds Peter put on a black block. The branch the bird sits on descends and catches a corner of the block. The branch is partially real, partially carved. Peter prefers to use brass, textured with acrylic modeling paste, for his branches. "I have absolute control this way. Otherwise I have to add and subtract pieces from a real branch, and I end up compromising the composition of the branch."

Peter decided against putting foliage on the branch. "I wanted the vignette look, so I left out anything that would take emphasis away from the bird."

Peter first carved the miniature grosbeak and then devised the base. He would have preferred to design the base first.

"The western flycatcher is a favorite of mine. It inhabits woodlands and forests and is only five and a half to six inches long. I often see these birds sitting in trees. I've found that if I see a bird flying off and returning to the same spot, it's usually a flycatcher. I wanted this bird to stand at the very top of the branch, its head twisted around, ready and unencumbered for its flying tricks."

The flycatcher is known for its small feet and wide beak, and both features must be accurately captured.

Peter built the branch out of brass and designed it to reflect the shape of the bird. "At first I was going to put greenery on the base, but I decided against it. I like the look of a simple vignette."

The western flycatcher's beak is hooked and, while Peter was carving, he snagged his shirt on the beak and broke it off. "To repair it, I inserted a wire into the end of the beak and built up the beak with baking soda and Super Glue. The baking soda acts as an accelerator and hardens like glue immediately. When the mix dries, it looks like clear Lucite. If painted properly, you can achieve a transparent look, just the way the top of a bird's beak is."

The singing fox sparrow sits on a branch that rests on an eight-sided base. The branch is sandblasted manzanita. Hemlock cones hang from the branch. "Each cone has a toothpick armature that I enclosed with an egg-shaped ball of Duro epoxy putty and detailed.

"In doing this piece, I discovered that by the time you seal the feet with lacquer, apply a coat of gesso, and then paint them, they have grown by twenty-five percent. Therefore, I make my feet smaller than the real thing, and they end up just right."

"I look at kingfishers a lot. I think they're a hard species to capture."

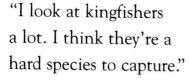

Peter has carved two belted kingfishers. "One has its beak open because I wanted to catch the noisy, raucous sound that the bird makes. I remember seeing a photo of an open-beaked kingfisher. The bird had its beak open maybe twenty degrees more than how I carved it. But I couldn't force myself to carve one like that." The tongue, a separate piece, is carved from tupelo.

To make the bird's ragged crest, he used a small rotary saw and then thin diamond and ruby carvers. "It's a difficult thing to do, but I think it looks effective. I don't see many others carved that I like."

To give the appearance that the bird is sitting up high, Peter placed it on a black block.

The other kingfisher sits up on a mossy snag and holds a crayfish in its mouth. Peter carved the crayfish and used copper wire for its legs. He made the moss from sponge rubber.

"My California quail composition is a basic bird sitting on a rock. This is what quail do. This bird is a strange and difficult one to carve, especially on a miniature scale. The head tends to get oversized, and I was constantly taking measurements for this carving to cut down on my errors."

To achieve the coloration, Peter used a combination of burning and staining with very light coats of acrylic.

The live bird.

"**E**ver since I saw a sora rail in Ocean City, Maryland, I've been enthusiastic about rails. The bird is almost always seen sneaking along on the ground or at water level. I didn't want the carving to sit at table level, so I put it up on a black block. I considered adding something tall in the habitat, but opted instead for two lily pads."

Peter uses a combination of burning and stoning on his birds. The magpie is ready for texturing. Most of the body, except for the fluffy feathers and parts of the wings, is burned.

"The animated pose
gives this piece
a feeling of motion."

To give a class of students an interesting and challenging project, Peter chose to have them do an open-winged nuthatch. This bird is nearly ready to be textured. The tail and wing feather separations have been pressed in with the side of a burning pen set low. Peter is particularly concerned with how he textures the surface of the wood prior to painting. In some cases, he burns and then applies a light coat of paint. "It is hard to put paint over a burned surface, especially in a light area such as the breast. Since primary and tail feathers for most birds are hard flight feathers, I usually burn them. The softer and fluffier feathers of the body I'll stone."

For some bird carvings, Peter uses a tiny, ball-shaped diamond bit, only a sixteenth of an inch in diameter, and makes depressions part way in from each soft feather edge to break up the surface and to create more textural diversity. He then goes back to the same areas with a slightly tapered, smooth white stone and stones each feather.

Sometimes Peter half carves, half paints a bird. A deep groove in the wood makes its own highlights and shadows. "I like to carve an area, making subtle depressions, and then paint in shadows. A good paint job can create lights and darks even on a flat surface."

"I do week-long seminars, and I like to offer a small bird project because students have trouble getting the bigger ones finished. The nuthatch is small enough for students to carve and paint in five days. Sometimes I wonder if the bird might be too small. I want to keep students interested, so I offer this bird with an open wing. Students love it."

The bird is in flight, coming vertically down a tree. Peter admits that the pose is more animated than real. "A bird has a fused backbone, but you can twist its head and tail. I did that so it would have a C shape. The animated pose gives this piece a feeling of motion, and the expressive position of the feet put energy into the carving."

"The open wing makes the project more complex, though it's unlikely you will see a bird in this position."

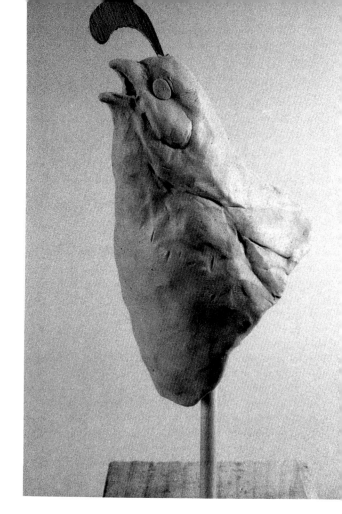

Peter uses a clay model to help pose a bird. "I use it to work out problems such as turning a head. I'll make the clay model the same shape as the bird I'm going to carve unless it's a bird I'm familiar with. Then I'll work the problems out in the wood. But with the clay, I use a wood armature and wrap that with wire to keep the clay from moving around."

He has also made mannequins with movable heads, wings, and tails so that he can work out various gestures. For the movable parts he uses stiff aluminum roof flashing that can be bent while retaining its shape.

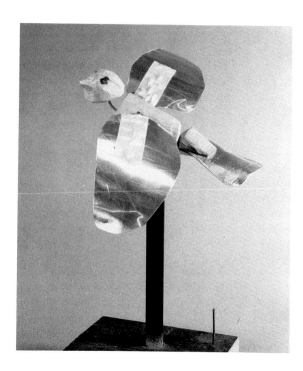

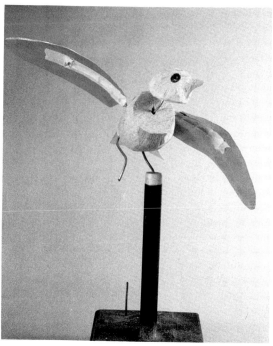

"I think it's important to sit down and analyze why a piece looks good, how the elements of design and composition work in a successful piece. I ask questions like: Does the piece have balance? Is it balanced symmetrically or asymmetrically? Was negative space considered in the composition? Where are shapes repeated in the piece? Were angles or textures repeated? Did warm and cool colors add to the feeling?"

Peter likes compositions that are simple and effective. His life-sized hermit thrush took a Best-in-Show at the California Open and a second in the open division for songbirds at the World Championships in 1986.

A sketch for a future composition—a woodpecker.

"I carved this belted
kingfisher with its beak open
because I wanted to catch
the noisy, raucous sound the
bird makes."

Peter has done kingfishers in a number of poses, birds with open beaks and birds holding their catch. "I saw a photo of a kingfisher with a crayfish in its mouth and thought it would be a great carving. It seemed to take no time at all, but it took Best-in-Show for miniatures at the 1987 Pacific Flyway Decoy Association Show in Sacramento, California."

"Robins have been special birds for me since childhood. They live in Gig Harbor all year long. I planned these robins for the 1988 Worlds. I wanted a V-shaped composition with a sculptural black block for a base. The piece captured Best-in-Category for miniatures at the 1988 World Championships."

Though a number of his miniature bird carvings have won him bests-in-show, Peter does not want to be classified as only a carver of miniatures. "I like to work that size and do what I want. I've done full-sized birds and very small ones. As a kid I did miniature models of detailed boats and anything else I was interested in. It's a nice size to work in."

Though he began carving basswood, he now uses only tupelo. "Tupelo is just right for small birds. It machines well and I can make it do what I want. I can work it cross-grained and the wood doesn't chip away, especially at the wing tips and beaks."

Even on a miniature scale, Peter is very precise with his measurements. "I used to say that if it looks right, it is right. But eight months down the line I'd see that the proportions were incorrect. Now, instead of making one-eighth-inch mistakes, the errors are down to a sixty-fourth of an inch."

"For this composition, I wanted to carve a miniature robin fluffed against the cold."

"I had originally wanted to carve these grosbeaks the year before. But grosbeaks, like cedar waxwings, are nomadic birds, and they didn't show up that spring.

"Since grosbeaks are seen in large groups, I decided to carve three instead of two. I first made a gesture drawing and then designed the piece around it. The arrangement of the birds follows the sweeping shape of the branch."

"I practically hand-feed grosbeaks in my backyard. I've seen as many as two hundred at one time. They are voracious eaters, especially of sunflower seeds. The bird has a stout beak, perfectly suited for seed eating."

"I decided on a C-shaped, or incomplete, circle. I wanted to mount the branch on something inconspicuous and decided on a black block. I might have elevated the design, but instead I have the branch descending off the block and onto the table. I'm pleased with the way the composition works.

"The branch is generic. I took one from my backyard and copied it using telescoping brass tubing. I like the strength I get from the tubing. I spent a great deal of time placing the birds in a characteristic position. They constantly squabble, and the males, in particular, fight. I've watched them at the feeders and in the trees, and they never let up."

One of the birds has its wings out. "I carved the bird from a single piece of tupelo. With a carving that small, you really can't hide joints, especially with plastic wood. I think one piece is the only way to go."

The composition took Best-in-Show at the Pacific Flyway Decoy Association Show in 1989 and a second at the Ward Foundation World Championships in the miniature division.

"I had difficulty with the shape of the bird. I felt uncomfortable making it so thin, especially when it's viewed from the front or rear, but rails are that way."

"I decided to feature the sora with a minimal base—just a black block with a lily pad on top." Peter makes his black, sculptural bases out of basswood. "Tupelo has edges so ripply you can't sand them perfectly. Tupelo is great for carving birds because birds are carved with lumps and bumps, but for bases, basswood is better."

At one time Peter sealed the block with lacquer, then applied gesso and black lacquer, but the black paint had a tendency to chip off, especially on the edges. Now he raises the grain by putting hot water on it and sanding it lightly. Then he applies a coat of black gesso. The block stays black, even if the finished surface chips.

"With this kind of base I can make the piece a vignette. The base not only raises up the bird but it also serves as a frame. Some painters use this approach. They start with a rectangular canvas and put into it only a few elements. They don't fill up the canvas."

The block works well because its geometric shape complements the shape of the bird. It adds lift and interest to the piece and makes a stylish presentation that took a second for open class miniatures at the 1989 Minnesota Masters Show.

"This varied thrush continued my experimentation with fat birds. Where I live, this bird is called the Alaskan robin. It's rarely found outside coniferous forests of the Pacific States and western Canada, measures nine to ten inches, and has a distinctive, orange breast. In winter, when the sun catches the breast, it's just like it's on fire."

"I decided on a vignette approach with the thrush, using a black block with an inverted branch. The piece won three awards in 1990: Best-in-Show at the Pacific Southwest Wildfowl Arts Show in San Diego and at the Pacific Flyway Decoy Association Show in Sacramento and a Best-in-Category at the Ward Foundation World Championships."

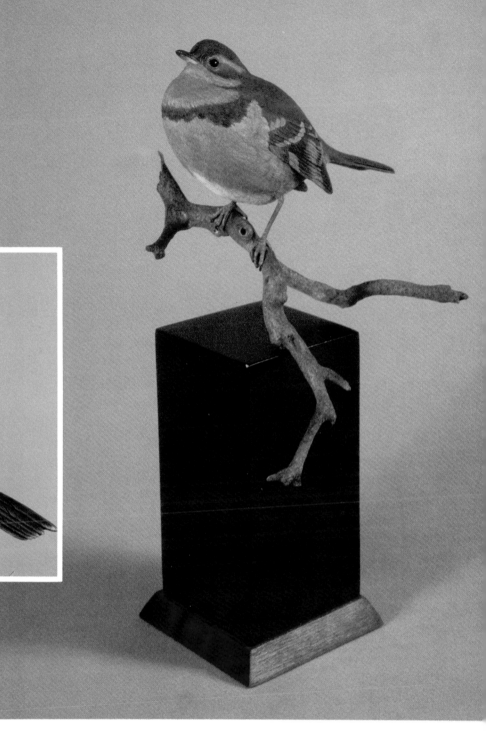

"Varied thrushes are shy, ghostlike, beautiful birds, and they have a haunting, flutelike call."

"**W**ith this one-half-life-sized California quail, I used one of my favorite positions: the sentry bird sitting high on something, ready to give the alarm."

"**N**ot in the characteristic upright pose, I posed this flycatcher on a branch that I assembled carefully of wood and then duplicated with brass tubing. The angles in the bird's posture are repeated over and over in the branch.

"Its feet are very expressive and contribute greatly to the piece's success."

The flycatcher took Best-in-Show in the open class of the 1989 Pacific Flyway Decoy Association Show.

"I love western flycatchers, and I often watch them in the spring and summer."

"**T**his nuthatch was designed and carved as part of a seminar. The class numbered ten students, and after they had completed their carvings, I accidentally broke off the bill from a piece done by a retired school teacher. I have yet to recover from the scathing look I received for doing that!"

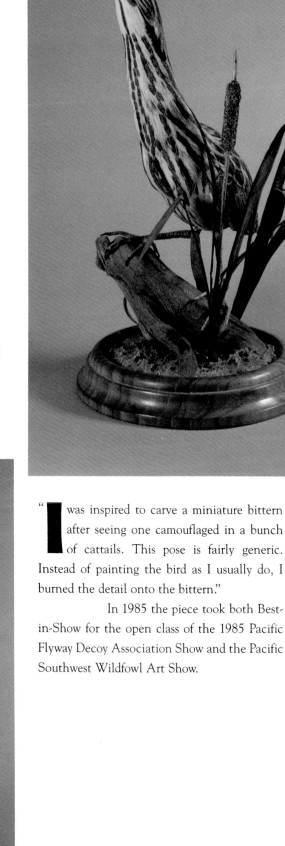

"I put in just enough cattails to indicate the habitat, but I didn't want to obscure the bird."

"I was inspired to carve a miniature bittern after seeing one camouflaged in a bunch of cattails. This pose is fairly generic. Instead of painting the bird as I usually do, I burned the detail onto the bittern."

In 1985 the piece took both Best-in-Show for the open class of the 1985 Pacific Flyway Decoy Association Show and the Pacific Southwest Wildfowl Art Show.

"In composing this waxwing, I used repeating shapes and colors to tie the composition together. The red berries on the branch match the red tips on the tertials. The intense color is very dramatic."

"Fox sparrows are yearly visitors to my house and are big, beautiful finches. To unify this piece, I repeated the angle of the bird in the branch several times. The sabal and hemlock cones show the extremely brushy and overgrown habitat this bird enjoys.

"Fox sparrows have very long hind claws, so I wanted to emphasize them. I had to make these feet three times, since they always seemed to grow by the time they were finished with several coats of paint. I finally learned that I had to make them smaller than I knew they were, and they turned out perfect."

The composition won Best-in-Show for the open class decorative life-sized division at the 1988 Pacific Southwest Wildlife Arts Show and took a second at the 1988 Ward Foundation World Championships for songbirds.

Peter spends time watching birds. "I've seen about sixty species come through the yard and to my feeders: spotted towhees, song sparrows, fox sparrows, house finches, chickadees, red-breasted nuthatches, and even sharp-shinned and Cooper's hawks.

"When I first moved to the woods of Gig Harbor, I saw hermit thrushes ghosting through the underbrush. Later that first winter, after a cold spell, I found one dead. I was quite upset. This carved hermit thrush still is special to me."

The composition won the decorative life-sized division of the 1986 Pacific Southwest Wildfowl Arts Show.

Leo Osborne

Art Without
Limits

He's been a fisherman, a shepherd, an auto pinstriper, a store clerk, a sign painter, and a surrealist. Today Leo Osborne ranks among the most versatile and gifted bird artists. Leo, who was born in Marshfield, Massachusetts, studied at the New England School of Art and Design. After graduation, he served for one year as art director of the *Cape Codder* newspaper in the 1960s. "Everybody I knew there sat around and talked about moving to the country. I decided to move to Maine." Leo built a geodesic dome in the woods and suffered through a bitter winter. He started painting, doing what he describes as inward and depressing pieces. He worked a number of jobs: salesman for Sears, mussel harvester, fish cutter. While he was working in the retail fish business, he carved an old lobster buoy, turning it into a sea duck. He painted signs and considered becoming a professional sign painter. He carved Beatrix Potter animals for his daughter Rachel. He lived on the farm and tended sheep and tried his hand at wildlife sketches. When he saw some bird carvings done by fellow New Englanders, he decided to try that as well.

His first birds were songbirds and he sold them for $125. By 1980, Leo knew he was ready to carve birds full-time. With the encouragement of two well-known Maine artists, Ted and Counselo Hanks, he sent pieces to the Waterfowl Festival in Easton, Maryland. All the birds sold. He began to exhibit in a local gallery. All these birds sold as well, and he was asked to do more. During the winter of 1982–83, he worked on a Canada goose. The day after he brought the goose to the gallery he got a call from one of the owners. The goose had sold for $10,000.

"I was trying to catch that moment in nature that's very dramatic. I didn't need to take a snapshot of it or sketch it, but I had the image of wrens and marshes in my mind and that is what I tried to create."

*S*ummer *Song*, a realistic piece done in 1984, depicts two marsh wrens on tall grasses made of copper. The bottom bird, a juvenile, is more sheltered than the upper bird, an adult wren.

"The concept for this piece came from the marshes of Warren. You look out over the field and see the marsh grass blowing. You can't create a whole bog, only a part of it, just the feeling of blowing grass."

Wanting the feeling of grasses that did not hide the birds, he gave the composition an airy look. The grass stems, wisping off in one direction, contributes a sense of motion.

"I did not want the grasses painted. If you put paint on metal, it looks as if you're hiding the metal. I wanted to enhance the character of the copper, so I chemically treated the metal to give it a green patina."

This piece was the first of his to be selected by the Leigh Yawkey Woodson Art Museum for their Birds in Art exhibit.

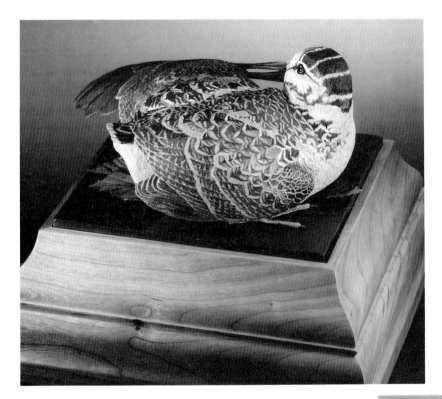

When Leo needed to turn a head, he would carve the head with a straight-on pose, cut it off, and turn it, a method practiced by many bird carvers. But he was not happy with the seam. He decided to carve this preening woodcock from one piece of wood and felt he was moving toward doing sculpture.

Even though the leaves are made from brown paper grocery bags coated with acrylics, the piece has a museum quality.

Instead of mounting *Preening* on a piece of driftwood, he put it on a piece of slate and an elevated pedestal that shows off the negative space created by the extended wing. "I like the pedestal approach. By minimizing the environmental elements, I can present birds like the woodcock as sculptures rather than habitat displays."

Pursuing work in natural wood, he conceived *Night Pursuit*, an owl swooping down on its prey. "I had acquired a white birch burl from a local bowl maker and the color of the wood and its shape reminded me of a snowy owl. I did very little sculpting on the wood; only the face and one foot with claws are detailed. The piece, sixteen inches in diameter, is approximately life-sized."

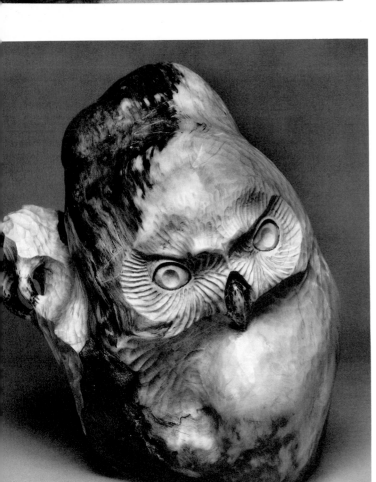

"The wood told me what to sculpt."

Leo has experimented with one-piece sculptures carved from tupelo. One carving, a storm petrel, is entitled *Wave Walker*. "Petrel" is derived from *Petros*, the Greek name for Peter, the disciple who tried to walk on water. Connected at three points—feet and beak—to the carved wave, the storm petrel does appear to walk on water. The bird looks as if it is dancing across the waves.

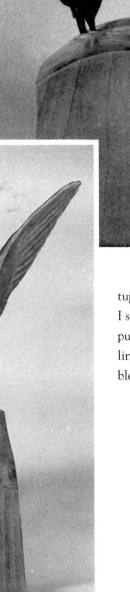

Leo stained the petrel. "The tupelo looked too blonde and colorless, so I stained it with washes of oil paint that I put on after I had saturated the wood with linseed oil so that the washes could be blended without streaking."

"I knew I had to carve peeps on a piece of the Maine coast."

Leo likes working in redwood burls. A burl is a growth that occurs on a tree. It has an erratic grain. "I purchase large pieces of burl and let them sit around the studio for a while until inspiration comes. Once I saw that the bumps on this piece of wood looked like barnacles and birds, I knew I had to carve the seven peeps on a piece of the Maine coast." The sculpture measures sixteen by twenty-four by thirty inches. *Peep Show* appeared in the 1987 Birds in Art Exhibit.

These redwood cormorants measure three feet high by three feet wide by twenty inches deep and weigh nearly one hundred pounds. One bird stands on a rock formation, and another below emerges from rock. The wings of the top bird droop down into the rocks and give the piece stability and strength. "There is an abstract quality to the wings. They appear bigger than life. They're an effective part of the overall composition."

In a piece like the cormorants, Leo is especially conscious of negative and positive space. "One creates the other. I'll take liberties to extend a wing farther than it can go naturally if it feels right. I don't worry about breaking an ornithological law. It's one of the first and best freedoms that man has: to be able to express himself artistically and not be hemmed in by strict laws and hampered by what someone else says.

"Rules are good to teach you in the beginning so you can learn what something is really like. After that you can break the rules. And to be a truly successful artist, I have to do just that.

"Many great abstract painters were exceptional draftsmen who could do realistic, detailed drawings. After learning the forms, they could then break the subject down to its abstract components. You cannot really go about it the other way, that is, be an abstractionist first. You must start with the skeletal structure and then learn to dissect it to its simplest form.

"Learn what there is to learn before you take the liberty of changing it. Van Gogh said to leave the obvious vague but exaggerate the essential. I believe that is true for sculpture."

"I don't worry about breaking an ornithological law. It's one of the first and best freedoms that man has."

W<i>ater's Edge</i> is one of three compositions Leo has done in which a single bird skims across water. For the first Leo made the base and bird separately. The bird was carved from basswood, the base from a cherry wood plank. A pin attached to the lower mandible secured the bird to the base. The second work was made from a single piece of cherry wood, the third from a single piece of redwood burl. As the bird skims the water, it leaves a wake. "I think the format of this composition has an abstract strength, and I enjoy seeing each of the three pieces photographed in black-and-white. I sculpted the third one so that it can be mounted on a wall, where it is even more dynamic and shows an even stronger sense of motion."

When Leo started carving, he put his birds on pieces of driftwood. Later he mounted them on carved stone. He tried putting a preening goose on a large rock with water as part of the habitat, but he felt the composition looked overdone. He wondered how the stones would look by themselves and decided to create stone sculptures without birds. Soon he started making glass boxes with carved stones set in them. The stones were light, and he was often asked how he was able to hollow out the rocks without leaving a seam.

Leo's early stones were basswood. For large rocks, he would laminate the wood and use a chain saw for the roughing out and grinders and gouges for the final roughing and for making crevices.

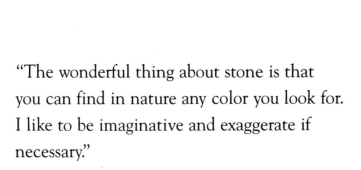

"The wonderful thing about stone is that you can find in nature any color you look for. I like to be imaginative and exaggerate if necessary."

Leo also made stone cliff faces. "They were large and I was afraid the wood might crack. I had to consider the weight and the expense of the wood. I soon began to experiment with foam. I create the textures on the foam with sponges and modeling paste. When this sets, I go over the surface with light sandpaper and then stipple acrylic paints on the surfaces. I won't spray on the paint because I want the rough, stone look. I enjoy the natural, nonuniform look of the freely painted surface."

For a gray stone, Leo applies Payne's gray, Mars black, and gesso. For a subtle sparkle he sometimes applies copper and bronze paints, as well as carmine reds and purples.

Recalling Jackson Pollack's technique, Leo will take a large brush and flick colors onto the rocks. "My wall sculptures are relatively smooth, but the different colors give the illusion of a granular appearance."

"I began to design the stone wall sculptures with birds in them. One composition, a red-breasted nuthatch foraging for food in a wall of granite, includes another element: the shadow of a sharp-shinned hawk. This profile shadow begs the question of whether the hawk has spotted the nuthatch. The shadow raised a lot of eyebrows."

This is an angular piece with the plane of two different rocks merging to the left. To the right the nuthatch is foraging for food as the shadow of the sharpshin moves toward it.

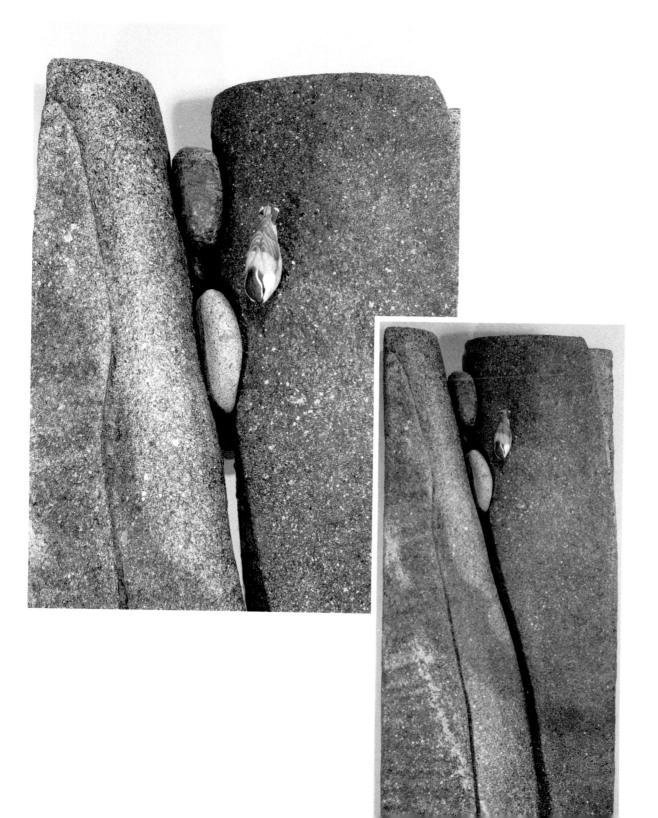

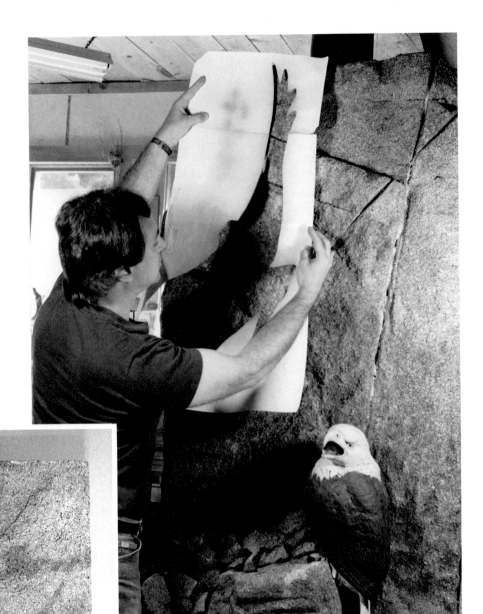

Leo spends a lot of time designing templates for these shadows. He wants a shadow to have motion and be abstract enough so that it doesn't look like the silhouette of a bird airbrushed onto the stone surface. He will frequently lift the template away from the stone so that the mist of the airbrush leaves a soft edge. If the bird is near the rock wall, he wants a hard edge. If far away, he will leave the shadow's edge less defined.

One stone wall piece has no carved birds. Instead, it has thirteen shadows of terns. "This is an intriguing piece. With no dimensional birds present, the viewer might not even notice the shadows."

I n *Peep Show* Leo creates a rocky shore covered with crags and barnacles. A group of tiny, peeping shorebirds clusters in the redwood burl. The birds are several species of shorebirds, all about the same size. When they are seen together, they are difficult to distinguish as they emerge from the stonelike burl.

"*Awakening* depicts a least tern slumbering in the recesses of an abstract form that I designed to give the feeling of an organic, human form. The tern is waking to the distant sound of an intruder."

In this painted piece titled *The Ploy*, the eggs in the camouflaged nest look like stones. What makes the piece sculptural and abstract is the broken wing emerging from the rock. Its features take on detail as the wing merges into the body.

"I think the piece is dramatic because of the flow of the wing, which leads the eye away from the eggs and up to the rest of the bird."

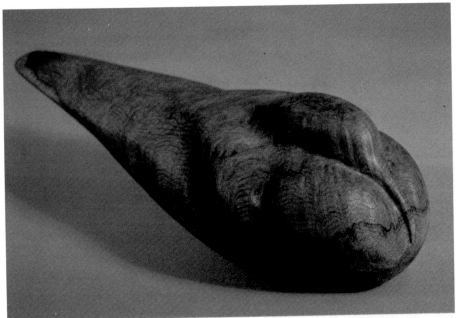

This solitary *Resting Shorebird* is carved from a piece of redwood burl. "I wanted to create something that would be wonderful to hold and would be of a shape so tactile that it would cry out to be held. This is a simple piece, elegant in its form and nature."

Blackhawk is a sweeping, spiraling composition twenty-eight inches high. Leo designed the piece so that it can be enlarged to five feet. "I did the piece using for the first time a unique, iridescent patina that I call the Blackhawk patina."

"Engineering this piece was most difficult. I wanted to create a dramatic sculpture and at the same time build a working fountain."

Black Ledge, Matinicus Island actually has water cycling through the crevice of the rock. "I feel the piece shows a sense of bird life and also the extremes of weather, water, and craggy rock forms. It's a total environment."

The inspiration for this large whooper swan came from a birch burl. "I remember seeing the sleeping form in the wood. This time though I made a clay model to help direct me through the sculpting." Although the light color of the wood complemented the bird, Leo gave it a light mist of a white-pigmented oil stain that he mixed with the finishing wax. "This gave a luminescent, almost lunar look and added to the mystical charm of the bird." Leo came up with the title, *Whooper Swan Awakening to Fly Off to the Moon*, while he was doing research for the piece. He learned that early Icelanders thought that after this great white swan nested it would fly off to the moon.

BENJAMIN MAGRO

Leo continues to experiment with new media and approaches to the art of wildfowl carving. He recently did an American kestrel in clay, then in wood. "I found that the carved bird looked stiff and lifeless by comparison, and I began to wonder why I was putting so much detail in my birds. When I work with clay, all my energies go right into the piece at the very moment of creation. But when I work with wood, I get caught up in all the detail and lose that creative flow."

BENJAMIN MAGRO

In *Water's Edge* a barn swallow dips in flight for a sip of water or a bug on the surface. The strong, abstract design works as a sculpture for the wall or table.

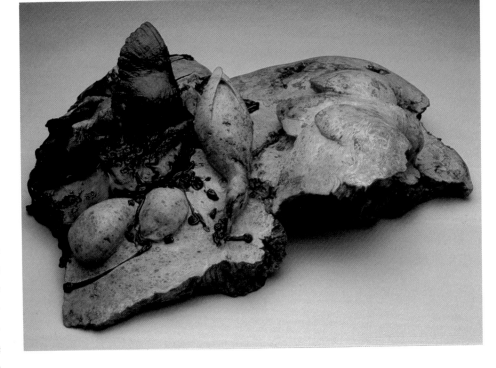

"I created this piece at the time the *Valdez* oil spill was occurring on Prince William Sound, Alaska. I was caught up in the horror of the event and wanted to do something to react to the nonreaction of the political bureaucracy. There are times when we as artists must make statements for that in which we believe. I titled the piece *Still Not Listening*."

"Near where swallows dwell, you can always see more swallows in flight. I wanted to show in the shadows of the incoming birds seen on this rocky ledge the busy comings and goings of the species. In the crevices of the black granite piece, a red-breasted nuthatch scurries around in search of food. The dynamics of lines and angles create a busy place for this bird and a sense of energy. I originally called this piece *Falling Rocks* but later retitled it *Black Rock Creek*."

BENJAMIN MAGRO

BENJAMIN MAGRO

A least tern sees its shadow on the rock. It's bringing a small fish to feed upon. Leo painted *Waterline* with barnacles to indicate the high tide level, where algae and sediment create a darkened line on the rock wall.

BENJAMIN MAGRO

Every year the kittiwakes return in pairs to the same *Breeding Cliff*. Here one mate rests from the long journey while the other guards the cliff dwelling from an approaching bird wanting to inhabit the same ledge.

Black and White, done in 1988, features razorbills, birds related to the puffin. Penguinlike, the razorbill measures sixteen to eighteen inches long and has a bladelike bill, a black back and head, and a white belly. Its habitat is the open ocean and it nests on cliffs and rocky shores.

Measuring four by six feet, this is one of Leo's largest pieces. An abstract, the piece emphasizes form and sculpture, not surface texture. "I placed the birds so that they are looking upward at the shadow cast by an incoming bird that will soon land in the space left open on the ledge.

"I took liberties with the painting, accenting high points with iridescence, though these birds have no such coloration. I used violets and blues to deepen the whites on the razorbills and reflect the colors in the stones up onto the birds."

"I wanted the black and white colors of the composition, not the fine details, to help make a statement."

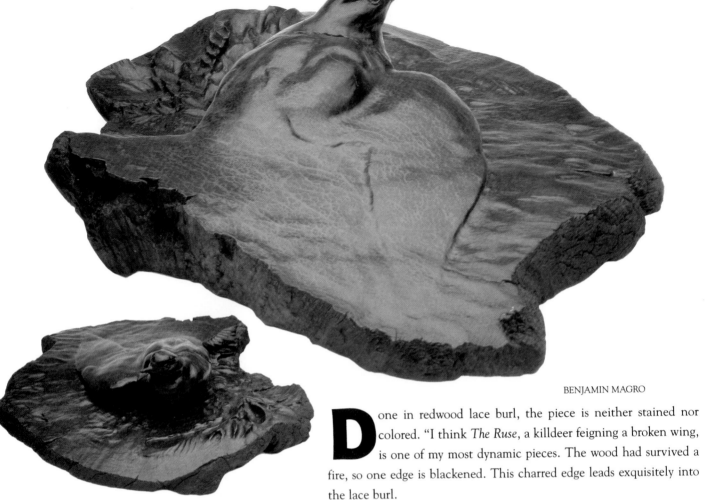

BENJAMIN MAGRO

Done in redwood lace burl, the piece is neither stained nor colored. "I think *The Ruse*, a killdeer feigning a broken wing, is one of my most dynamic pieces. The wood had survived a fire, so one edge is blackened. This charred edge leads exquisitely into the lace burl.

"The wood grain has nothing to do with killdeer markings. The bird is down near the ground, hiding, and I wanted the lacy look to help make the bird look inconspicuous."

Leo has done two more feigning killdeer in natural woods, one in redwood burl and the other in a maple bird's-eye burl. "I wanted to see how far I could take the same subject and make it work again."

The redwood burl from which this Best-in-World winner for interpretive wood sculpture was carved had sat untouched in Leo's studio for two years. "The burl was too heavy to move around, so I cut the top off and discovered a sleeping goose in the wood. It is titled *Gentle Rest*.

"There was an area of wood at the base that looked like a webbed foot. I thought it looked like the form of a sitting goose, and the grain suggested a turned neck with the head on the back. I like the process of letting the wood speak for itself. Patience is a virtue, and I do not force myself on the wood."

Leo sculpted this woodcock on stone from a single block of wood. The piece is titled *Intimidated*. Leo wonders is it the bird looking up at the intruder who is intimidated, or are we, the intruders, the intimidated?

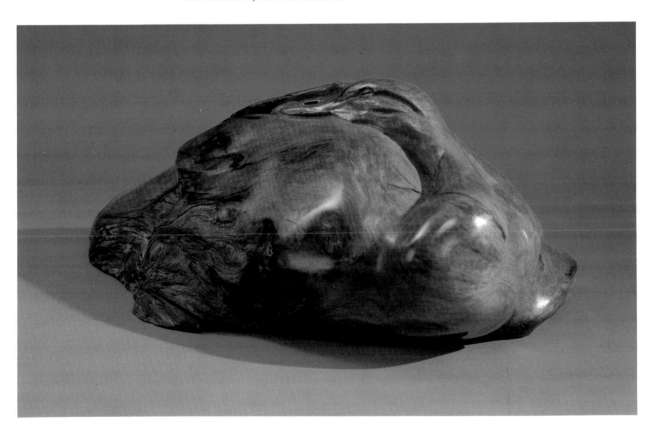

Leo carved the twenty-four-inch piece from a single burl of maple. A barn owl emerges from and circles around a pedestal base. "*The Orator*—an owl—stands upon his soapbox and preaches his words of avian wisdom to us."

The Vision Keepers measures twenty-six inches by twenty-six inches. The carved and painted black-billed magpie is attached to a buffalo skull by the horn. "To me, these two—the live black-billed magpie and the remaining skull of the buffalo—are watchers and keepers of the Native American way of life."

Floyd Scholz

Orchestrating Balance And Harmony

When Floyd was fifteen, he was invited to exhibit at the Remington Gun Club in Stratford, Connecticut. He had been carving for five years, and he brought several pieces—waterfowl, life-sized and miniature, and his favorite bird, the mallard drake. "I did not approach carving as a decoy maker, like my uncle who taught me. I loved the diorama approach of putting birds into meaningful settings. I went to the Connecticut Audubon Society's bird carving show in Fairfield, Connecticut, in 1975 when I was seventeen years old and met John Scheeler. Few people were doing raptors, even songbirds were very new. The focus was still on waterfowl, seabirds, and shorebirds." Because Floyd was interested in wood, he decided to pursue a career as an industrial arts teacher. But he loved track and field as well. In college he was a three-time All American and a member of the U.S. track team, so he had little time for bird carving. Between 1975 and 1979, he carved only four birds.

Floyd earned a Bachelor of Science degree in industrial education, but he wasn't ready to begin a career in a school shop. He took off for Vermont and spent two years building houses. In his free time, he carved and began selling his work. Soon he was making as much money selling songbirds and hawks as he was building houses.

Floyd went to his first competition, the U.S. National Decoy Show, in 1983. His bird won Best-in-Show in the amateur class. For the first time since he had begun carving, he considered the possibility of making a living carving birds.

217

TAD MERRICK

For this composition of five puffins, Floyd spent three months researching the birds and 1,000 hours carving and painting them. Floyd wanted to enter the 1986 World Championships with a sizable and impressive composition. He considered doing three ring-billed seagulls fighting for a clam. "I carried the idea through to Styrofoam models, but I hit a wall in that three birds of the same color and size seemed like a dead end. I felt I had to change direction, and I remembered that a friend, Dr. Stephen Kress of Cornell University, had been establishing breeding colonies of puffins on Matinious Rock off the coast of Maine. I hadn't seen another carving of a puffin, and I thought a composition of these birds would be unique. Puffins are smaller than ring-billed gulls, so I upped the number of birds to five. Since puffins prefer to live in colonies, five is not an unreasonable number."

Given the way puffins behave, Floyd could have designed the piece a number of ways. After spending weeks doing sketches, he decided on a composition that brought the five puffins together in a spiral. As the design evolved, he became more intrigued with the idea of implying motion in the composition while at the same time portraying the rocky habitat so common along the coast and islands of Maine.

"I wanted to carry the piece beyond the puffins so I introduced a crab. Green crabs climb up on rocks, even where puffins reside, so the two very different species share the same environment. I filmed and studied live crabs so I could accurately portray the leg sequence and ensure the correct appearance of movement.

"I wanted the crab to look as if it were skittering across the rocks, raising and lowering its legs. The crab is an interloper, it crosses the rock face below the birds. The puffin closest to the crab and lowest in the composition balances on one foot, indicating motion. Another bird, higher up, is curious but less tense, sure that there is no threat. The other three puffins are out of the zone of action and bring the viewer's eye up to the top of the rocks in a spiral motion. The piece has a geometry that keeps the eye from drifting."

The rocks are enclosed in an octagonal base except for one rock that spills over. "I never saw anyone take a rock off the base before. It added a unique twist to the composition."

I n this composition a puffin is the prey of an Arctic gyrfalcon. Floyd chose the white-phase gyrfalcon because the white and black markings complement the black and white colors of the puffin, and the yellow of the gyrfalcon's feet and cere complement the orange of the puffin's beak and feet.

For this project Floyd did research at the raptor rehabilitation center at Cornell University in Ithaca, New York, and consulted with Dr. Kress.

"There are three planes in the composition: one for the falcon, which is looking up and to the left, another for the dead puffin, and a third for the tundra rock, which ties everything together by going down and to the right. The rock is the unifying mass of the whole piece. It acts as the launch pad.

"I planned this design so that the rock is a convergent point where the planes come together, thereby creating a point of origin. I hollowed out the rock, which is made of basswood, to minimize the chance of its cracking or checking. Next I covered the rock with fiberglass screening and Duro Rock Hard Water Putty and stippled the putty with a half-inch-wide bristle brush to achieve a pebbly surface. Finally, I made minor cracks and splits on the surface with a knife."

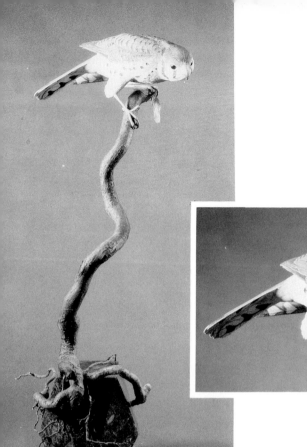

"A composition like this one is a series of problem-solving exercises. Where are the feet when the bird is in this position? Where is the balance point? At what angles are the bones? What about the position of the wings?"

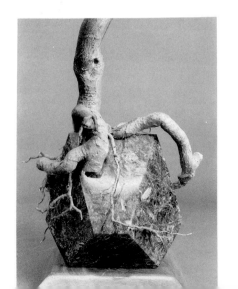

A kestrel hovers when in flight, so Floyd placed the bird on a twisty branch to reflect this flight pattern. For prey he chose the dragonfly because its mass works well with the kestrel. "Both the kestrel and the dragonfly are phenomenal fliers, so it is a duel between these two. This time, the kestrel won."

The kestrel stands twenty-three inches above the base. "I relied on my sense of proportion to determine the height of the piece. But for help I made a Styrofoam model of the kestrel and moved it up and down the branch, which was longer than that of the finished composition, until I found a balance of height and mass. More often than not, I rely on my eye for what will work and what won't."

The base is a piece of verd antique marble quarried near Floyd's farm in Hancock, Vermont. The marble, which is rich with green and white streaks, is faceted and polished. "Using the marble was like adding a large jewel to the composition. It contrasted well with the roughness of the branch that entwines the marble."

"**M**usic and the visual arts are more related than most people think. When I look at a well-orchestrated piece of art, I hear music. When I design a piece, I think of highs and lows and a midrange. A good bird composition has to flow with a lyrical undercurrent. And like an orchestra, a well-thought-out composition is the sum of the parts. In the case of a bird sculpture, it's anatomy and color, physical harmony, and balance. Every aspect of the composition should be complementary and not compete with the other elements."

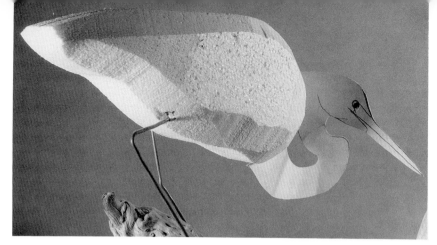

"One of my most successfully orchestrated pieces is a pair of snowy egrets, titled *Everglades Dancers*, which I did in 1987. Snowy egrets, in my view, epitomize the elegance and grace so common in the bird world. I wanted to portray them in a way that would allow the viewer to feel as if these two birds were performing a ballet. I designed the sculpture as a composer would have orchestrated a symphony.

"I was continually putting together the composition as I was carving the birds so I was able to achieve a better idea of how it would go together. The legs are quarter-inch-diameter brass rods. The lower egret's wings are stoned, textured, and burned."

Floyd used Styrofoam and paper to model the upper egret and wood, paper, and clay for the lower one. The dowel rod allowed him to try different poses by altering the axis of the body.

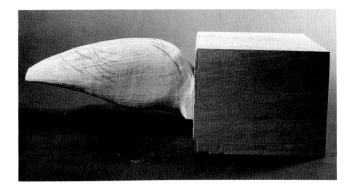

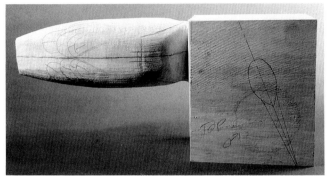

"All the elements had to work with one another: the bass, midrange, the highs and lows, all the parts working together to make the whole piece complete."

The upper egret was carved from one block of tupelo with extra wood for the neck and head. Care had to be taken because the beak of the top bird was cross-grained, making it susceptible to breaking. Floyd used a small, round ruby carver to ripple the feathers prior to burning. He tried many materials for the plumage before he settled on copper filament wire from a motor armature.

By carefully positioning the top bird's wings and emphasizing body posture, Floyd was able to impart a sense of motion and harmony in the composition.

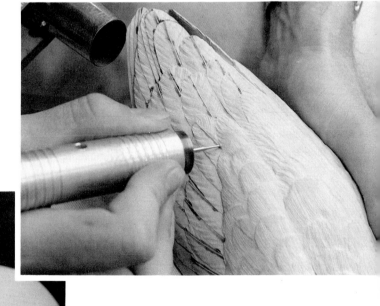

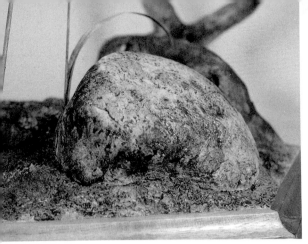

The pheasant spirals upward to the left, giving the piece direction and motion. Careful blending and brushwork are essential for duplicating the individual breast feathers.

In 1988 Floyd created a composition of flight and power when he put a ring-necked pheasant into the air. He was commissioned to carve the bird by collector Michael Kane of Nantucket Island, Massachusetts. "Michael was very specific in what he wanted. This is one of the real challenges and, at times, difficulties in accepting commissions. It means working with a client to develop an idea that we can both agree on. Michael really liked the compositional works of the seventies and eighties, the ones with dirt, rocks, leaves, and other habitat, and he wanted the pheasant to be displayed with those elements.

"I designed the flying bird with its wings in the downstroke so that it is fighting the force of gravity. I wanted to show opposing forces, one being gravity, the other the force of muscles and feathers. I've orchestrated that struggle through the breast. That's where you can see the tension."

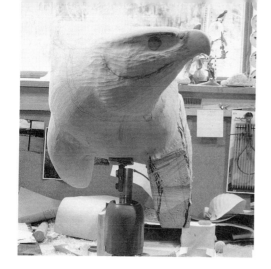

"The bald eagle is overwhelmingly big, as large as thirty-five to forty inches, with a wingspan of seven feet. I started with the head. I felt if I got the head right, I knew that the rest would fall into place."

Floyd perched the bald eagle low and spread its wings. "I wanted this eagle to have forward movement, so I angled the bird over to one side and curved the back a bit to give the bird that forward thrust. To add to the thrust, I altered the height of the wings. Carving both wings in identical positions would have made the bird look angelic."

Before inserting the wings into the body, he made tenons at their insertion points, put slots in the tenons, and drove hardwood wedges into the slots. As he pushed the wings into the body, the wedges spread the tenons apart. For extra measure he doweled them through the body.

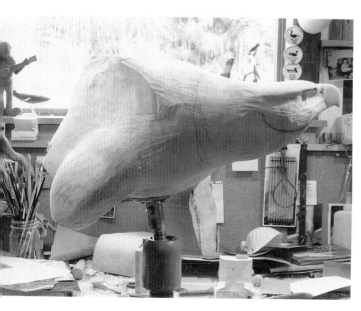

The live bird.

"I titled the piece *Approaching Storm* because this mighty aerial predator looks as if it's about to hurtle off a cliff face into the building winds of an approaching storm. But the title has a dual meaning. The future of these great birds is stormy. Their habitat is being destroyed.

"For doing birds as large as an eagle, I find a chain saw helpful. I thought it was sacrilegious to use one, but when I was doing the bald eagle, I knew I had to shape the wings from solid blocks of wood. I thought of the many days it would take to chisel away all the waste wood and I bought a chain saw, refiled the teeth so that they were almost straight across instead of angled, so I could chip out rather than shear the wood. In two hours I had a large block of tupelo sculpted into the shape of a wing."

The inspiration for this red-tailed hawk, titled *Windago*, came one snowy Vermont day in 1988. "I was riding a ski lift up a mountain and saw a red-tailed hawk attempting to land in the upper branches of a long-dead elm tree. As the large raptor landed, it was suddenly caught off balance by a strong gust of wind. Shifting its body weight and fanning its tail, the raptor opened its left wing and revealed a silvery white underwing. The entire sequence of events lasted just five seconds, but the bird's nimbleness and grace stayed with me. I had to tell that story in a wood sculpture."

TAD MERRICK

TAD MERRICK

TAD MERRICK

TAD MERRICK

"**T**o really tell the story I felt I had to create a strong sense of design from the bottom of the base up through to the top of the bird's head. I sculpted an abstract base and carved a weathered branch to flow off the base to suggest the wind. I like this style of combining the abstract and real."

At heart Floyd is a serious conservationist who is disgusted with the way man has been systematically altering the landscape and destroying the animal world. "When I create a composition, I try to imagine the orchestrated, natural balance that occurred thousands of years before man dominated this planet."

Floyd does a variety of birds, including songbirds. He designed a bluebird composition to impart a sense of motion. "Blink your eye and the bird is gone. The twist of the head, the slight opening of the left wing, and the flair of the tail all fit together to tell a story of movement."

Floyd has carved several hummingbirds, all in flight and mounted on flowers.

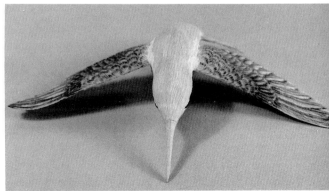

"I wanted this great horned owl, called the tiger of the woods, to look like a portrait of a king, the lord of the forest. The stately look comes in part from the robust chest, the position of the left foot, and the intense look in the eyes. 'This is a bird you don't mess with' is the statement I was going for."

Floyd put another bird in the composition: a blue jay. It harasses the owl but does not come within striking distance. The owl's laid-back ear tufts show the irritation it feels.

The composition is designed in the shape of an X. By visually extending the line of spruce branch the jay sits on, the viewer finds that it crosses the center of the owl.

"I like to put more tension into a piece by putting the bird to one side of center. The brain says that the bird should be at the center of the base, but to offset it is to put the bird in motion."

> "I like to put more tension into a piece by putting the bird to one side of center."

The live bird.

TAD MERRICK

"I poised this American bald eagle for flight. Drawing on my experiences working as a volunteer with the Peregrine Fund, I observed these birds of prey and learned firsthand that they have unparalleled flying skills. As the winds pick up prior to a summer thunderstorm, the eagles would become quite excited. They would ride the wind currents seemingly for the sheer pleasure of demonstrating their freedom.

"I intended the rock mass beneath the bird to represent a cliff outcropping. Since it is the exact shape of the bird's body, it acts as a shadow."

Floyd spent 1,200 hours—more than seven months—on this piece. "Shaping, sanding, and wood burning a work this size is a true test."

TAD MERRICK

" I designed and carved this sculpture for the sheer pleasure of telling a story. A white-phase Arctic gyrfalcon's keen eyes pick up the frantic wingbeats of an Atlantic puffin heading toward the coast. In pursuit, the hungry falcon quickly narrows the distance until, with an explosion of feathers, the quarry is snatched from the air and carried off to a rocky ledge to be plucked and eaten.

"Painting an all-white bird is a real challenge. I did a great deal of underpainting and blending of warm and cool colors to show softness and depth in both the falcon and the puffin. For the whites I used straight gesso and added small amounts of burnt umber."

"Thanks to the dedication and hard work of Dr. Steve Kress of Cornell University, who heads the Puffin Project on several islands off the Maine coast, I was fortunate to be able to spend time on these islands as a volunteer for the project, and I have a great love for these sea parrots. In my sculpture *The Return of Little Brother*, I wanted to portray the male Atlantic Puffin standing proud upon the granite rocks under which eggs are laid.

"The jet-black plumage contrasts sharply with the soft-white breast and belly. To simulate soft feathers overlapping hard-edged feathers, I made single brush strokes and highlighted the overlapping areas.

"Pose and attitude speak volumes. The position of the head indicates that this puffin is watching the skies, perhaps for the return of his mate.

"The brightly colored bill and triangular eye scales are present only during the breeding season and are shed as the postbreeding puffins head back out to sea for six months. I used acrylic paints and many thin wash coats to get bright yet soft colors."

"I wanted an optimistic sculpture that would say, 'Despite a rather sad and brutal past, the future for the Atlantic puffin looks bright.'"

Kestrels are a popular subject because they are relatively small and beautifully colored. In *Caught on the Wing*, a tall, twisting branch gives a feeling of height. Floyd chose verd antique marble for the base because of its unique color and patterns.

"The dragonfly wings were a challenge. I made them of heat-sensitive Mylar film, scribed them with a diamond stylist to show the veins, and washed them with black India ink.

"I used a combination of stoning and burning techniques to carve the various types of feathers. Generally, I stoned the soft-edged feathers of the breast and belly and burned the hard-edged flight, tail, and back feathers."

"My close friend and fellow bird lover, Dr. Myron Yanoff, once quipped that, as a child growing up in Philadelphia, his only exposure to bird life were the house sparrows. At his request I carved *Urban Survivor*. With no specific design plan I began carving a block of tupelo and let the bird emerge on its own. It came forth in a highly animated way."

Except for the flight feathers, Floyd stoned the whole body surface using a small, white Arkansas cylinder and a small diamond ball for feathering around the eyes. A stoned surface lends itself to more-detailed brushwork than a burned surface. Earth-toned paints are usually the easiest to make look soft and realistic.

" Everglades Dancers is what developed after a two-week research trip into the Florida Everglades and visits to Ding Darling Wildlife Sanctuary. I had a commission for a pair of egrets, and I wanted a work that would personify grace and dignity. This pair seems to dance down the trailing mangrove root. The verd antique marble base shimmers emerald, the color of the jewellike swamp water."

First Floyd made a clay model of both birds to work out the technical aspects of the piece. He had to develop special techniques to make the flowing plumes. Using a carbide stump cutter, he roughed out the neck and head areas and did lots of sanding by hand. Establishing center lines during the carving process helped him maintain symmetry in the neck.

For birds with long, slender bills and thin tail feathers, he uses tupelo because it's a stable wood that doesn't warp.

Greg Woodard

*A Love
For Raptors*

Greg Woodard of Ogden, Utah, seemed destined to carve birds. His father was a cabinetmaker and a wood shop teacher who taught his students furniture making and bird carving. Greg remembers seeing a bird carving in Jackson, Wyoming, and hearing his father comment that there are people who carve for a living. Greg was listening.

As a young boy he loved watching Walt Disney specials, especially those on falconry. He remembers his first real experience with a live bird of prey. In 1973 he discovered an eagle's nest near his family's cabin and spent his free time that summer watching the young birds until they fledged.

After Greg graduated from high school, he worked a number of jobs. He built houses, did cabinetry, and worked for the Union Pacific Railroad. During the winter months he started carving birds. He had no contact with other bird carvers, and he experimented on his own with tools and surfaces. He did a ruddy duck in 1981, his first waterfowl, and later that year he made a canvasback. These were smooth birds carved in white pine with wide lines to represent the barb lines. By the time he had done his fourth bird, a Canada goose, he was carving in feathers, texturing the surface, and staining the wood.

"I decided to try burning
because it seemed
the burner was a natural
for making texture."

In 1985 Greg carved a shoveler duck. He had a study mount that he scrutinized. He counted every feather he could see on the mount then carved feathers on the surface and burned in the barb lines. "I was still learning on my own, out of touch with other carvers, but I decided to try burning because it seemed the burner was a natural for making texture."

He heard about a carving club that met in Bountiful, Utah, and decided to attend. He brought along his shoveler. Lance Turner, a carver who had placed among the top three in the decorative miniatures at the World Championships, was lecturing that evening, and during the course of his talk, he kept referring to Greg's shoveler. Lance told Greg that he should be showing his birds professionally and entering competitions.

hough Greg's family was against his carving full-time, he continued to devote more and more time to it. He found that carving raptors was more satisfying than doing waterfowl.

He became an apprentice falconer and began to fly and own raptors and use them as references. He did a number of birds of prey—gyrfalcons, peregrines, and prairie falcons.

It's difficult to tell Greg's carvings from live birds.

The live peregrine.

The carved peregrine.

A carved prairie falcon.

The sketch.

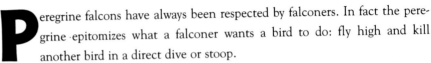

"The peregrine is a
confident bird,
and I try to make it
look that way."

Peregrine falcons have always been respected by falconers. In fact the peregrine epitomizes what a falconer wants a bird to do: fly high and kill another bird in a direct dive or stoop.

Using a captive-bred peregrine falcon, Greg had to get it to adapt to people, motion, noise, and even other animals. "A peregrine will adjust to most anything, even a household pet, but it has a strong cry that may be hard to tolerate. I know more about this bird than any other raptor. The mature peregrine is beautifully colored with a black cap and white cheeks. It's slate-blue back and spade and barred chest make it more colorful than other raptors."

Greg places his peregrines on rocks and carves both the bird and the rock from a single piece of tupelo. "The bird blends right into the rock. I like this way of carving. It's more natural, more durable, and it's sculpturally sound. I think it also makes the piece more valuable."

In this piece, Greg wanted the bird to be crouching as if there were an eagle flying overhead. The peregrine is keeping its eyes on what is overhead.

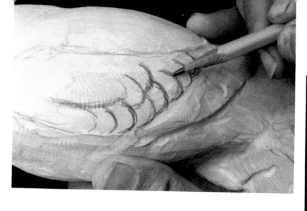

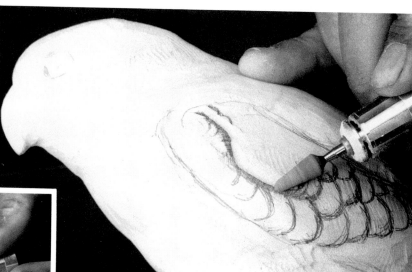

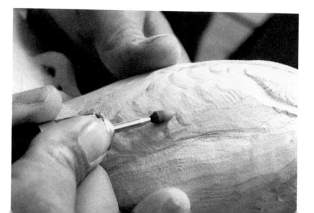

The texture of feathers can be quite different. Soft breast feathers tend to be small and almost hairy looking, while the harder, stiffer wing and tail feathers appear more prominent. To achieve the soft look, Greg uses an abrasive point or texturing stone. For the rigid feathers of wing and tail, it's the burning pen.

When Greg started carving, he cut in every feather he could see and burned every barb line with a burning pen, whether they were breast or primary feathers. Now he stones in lines on all the feathers regardless of whether they are soft or hard.

Greg's first step in preparing to texture the surface of one of his raptors is drawing in the feather patterns on the upper wing coverts. He then outlines the feather groups with a Dremel stone, one that can be reshaped and resharpened if necessary. For small feathers, he outlines with a smaller, sharper stone. He then goes over the stoning with sandpaper.

"I stone in lines on all the feathers regardless of whether they are soft or hard."

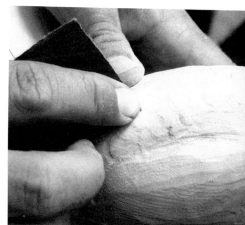

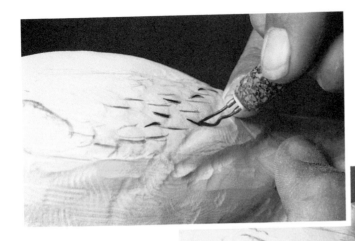

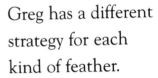

Greg has a different strategy for each kind of feather.

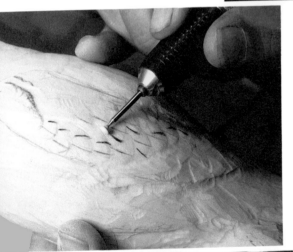

Next he draws in shafts and feather splits. Greg uses a burning pen to make the shafts. He then goes back and cleans up the splits with a pointed white stone. For the stiff barbs he uses a sharp, cone-shaped abrasive stone.

Greg bases his strategy on how he sees the feathers. Wing, back, and tail feathers he observes as being hard. But the breast feathers he views as being almost furry in appearance. He uses a cylindrical stone on the breast but burns in the shafts of these feathers. For the hard feathers, he stones and then partially burns over the stone lines.

He uses a disk-shaped stone for the hard lines. It makes a cut like a burning tip. Why doesn't he just burn? "The burning pen does not leave a clean enough surface for the paint to be applied later. But I do go over the stone lines with a burning pen set at a low temperature. I find this technique gives me a harder, stiffer-looking feather."

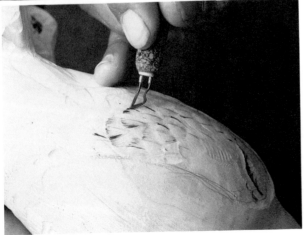

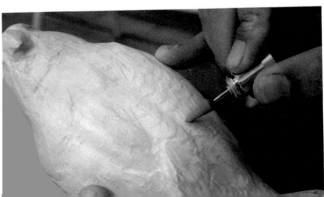

reg's texturing strategy is to burn part of each feather as a way of tightening up the stoning lines at the outer edge and at the base of the quill line. To do this, he works with a burning pen first from the edge, lifting up the tip near the center. Then he turns the bird around in his hand and works from the quill toward the middle, lifting the pen before he reaches the center of the feather. Using a large Dremel stone, he prepares the surface of the breast. He makes not only lumps and bumps but also grooves and splits.

"I want to create almost a wild look, one that is soft and hairy yet fluid."

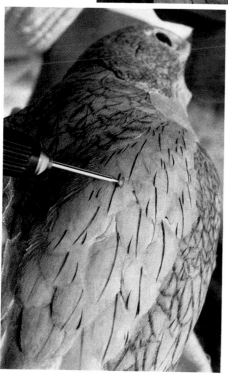

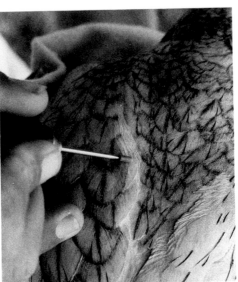

To burn over the stone lines, Greg keeps the burner at a very low setting so that no char lines result. He makes two strokes from the quill, which he has burned in, out toward the edge, and then from the edge of the feather in toward the quill. But he does not go the full distance from quill to edge and edge to quill. Instead, he releases the pressure on the tip so that there is a subtle transition that leaves the center of each feather with half a stone line. The feathers look fuller and softer because of that pressure release. Another reason for burning is that he can get closer to the quill line with a burning tip than with a stone, no matter how small it is.

When he paints, he does each feather in halves, painting from the quill outward. All this combines to give each feather its two subtle curvatures.

Greg uses a burning pen to raise back feathers.

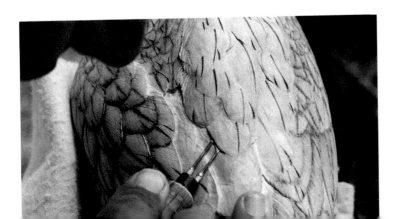

owny feathers can protrude on the back of the bird. He defines these and the hair-like feathers around the eyes and the soft feathers on the front of the head with a cylindrical stone. He uses a fine-pointed stone to make the scales on the feet.

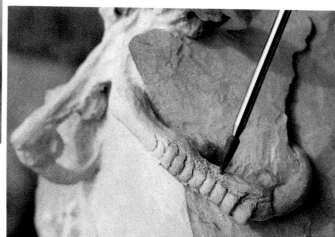

Though many carvers paint with acrylics, Greg prefers oils. In Utah's dry climate acrylics dry too rapidly. But the overriding reason he chooses oils is that he feels acrylics look brighter, but oils look richer.

"The thinner you paint, the more the paint looks like a stain. I stain the wood and build paint on that. On the back of a bird like the peregrine, I want the paint to be thin so that the burning I do is not filled up. On the front of the bird, I want the paint to make the stoned surface looked softer than it really is."

On the white breast of the peregrine Greg emphasizes highlights and shadows. Assuming a light source coming from above and in front of the left shoulder of the bird, he uses warm colors there, and on the lower right he applies cool colors. Starting with the cool colors, he applies ultramarine blue, which gives shadows and emphasizes depressions.

To warm up areas and emphasize bumps, especially on the upper breast, Greg uses warm colors—yellow, orange, red, and green.

"Blocking in this broad spectrum of colors will appear loud until I later apply layers of white to subdue them. I also tie the variety of colors together by applying a very light sienna color."

Though Greg could use a titanium white thinned with turpentine, he prefers to mix it with an alkyd white to speed the drying time. "The first coat is thin and fairly wet, and I leave it wet so that the other colors will blend with the white. After coating the entire bird with the white, I start warming up the left side of the bird with yellows and cooling off the right side with blues.

"I like to make the breast colorful. One carver told me that he could see every color of the rainbow on the breast of my white-phase gyrfalcon. I can lighten up all those colors by putting the white on more heavily, or I can darken areas with colors like burnt sienna. A wash will tone down the brighter colors. Orange is a good color for the transitional area between cool and warm areas."

"When you run a wash over oil, you have to be careful that the oils have dried for a few days or you'll get a muddy mess."

With feathers, most color is toward the center, while the edges are lighter. When painting a feather, if most of it shows, Greg paints a lighter color toward the top of the feather. Where it underlaps another feather, there is a depression, which he paints cooler.

The foot clutching the rock was carved as part of the rock. The other foot was inserted.

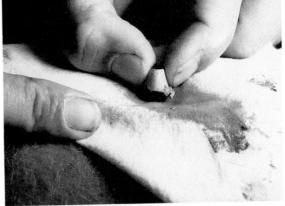

"Because I make the raptor's eyes, I can make one darker than the other. And I can paint lines across the eyes to represent the shadow of the brow."

Working apart from other carvers, Greg had never heard about taxidermy eyes. He always made his own. First he used the ends of dowels that he rounded off and painted with enamel to give them a shiny look. Then he began to experiment with Plexiglas.

Still using a painted dowel that he left flat, he places a Plexiglas lens over each eye. The lens starts out as a flat cutout that fits over the dowel. He puts the dowel and the lens into a drill press and files the lens round as the dowel is spinning. Using a metal file for the shaping, he then sands the Plexiglas with 220-grit and 320-grit sandpaper. In the final step he uses a polishing compound to remove any scratches.

"A raptor's eyes are not round. I can make a slightly elongated eye and get the shape I want without having to use putty over a glass eye. Glass eyes are usually a solid color, but a raptor's eyes have many darks and lights—variations of colors. You can even see muscles." Most carvers who use glass eyes paint the bird with the eyes in place because paint can be scraped off the glass without damaging it. With Plexiglas, which is much softer than glass, Greg must take the eyes out of their sockets before he applies oils. To remove one eye, he drills a hole in the back of the head straight through to the eye socket. He can then insert a wire and push out the eye. Instead of making another hole for the other eye, he makes a channel between the two eye sockets through which he can push out the other eye.

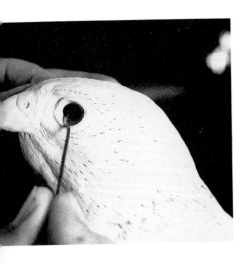

"The gyrfalcon is an intelligent bird, one that can look both comfortable and aggressive. It has such an intense stare, and it's smart enough to know what's coming up on it. That's what I wanted to capture with my carving."

"Only the emperor could fly a gyrfalcon. The biggest and most powerful falcon, it has traditionally been flown high overhead while the quarry is flushed out by dogs. Gyrfalcons don't fly very high, but they are fast. They can chase down a duck, something not many birds can do."

Greg posed the white-phase gyrfalcon to look comfortable. The body is fluffed out, and it looks twice the size of an alert or tense bird. The head is pivoted to reflect the spiraling branch. "The bird seems to be aware of something. There could be a predator coming up on it. It's not scared, but the eyes are focused."

Both the stump the gyrfalcon rests on and the bird itself are carved from a single piece of tupelo. The only separate pieces are the primaries and the one foot that is tucked up in the breast. "The tail is too straight down on the bird for the primaries to lay flat on it, and it made for a better anatomical detailing to make a separate foot."

Though Greg is more comfortable carving rocks, he felt the colors of a stump better complemented the colors of the gyrfalcon. The next gyrfalcon he carved is on a rock.

Both the stump the gyrfalcon rests on and the bird itself are carved from a single piece of tupelo.

"I wanted the branch to look as if it had been blown apart by the speed of the passing merlin."

"I always wanted to do a flying raptor, and I thought a falcon would be the best because it has an aerodynamic look. Like other falcons, this bird is designed for intercepting birds in flight. It is swift and agile, and it can outmaneuver something as quick as a dragonfly. But small birds are their primary sources of food.

"Originally I wanted to do a peregrine chasing a duck, but I did not have enough time. So I chose a much smaller bird—the merlin. I thought a junco would be a good choice of prey because its colors would not overpower the merlin's."

Greg first designed the piece so that the merlin's feet were out ready to grab the junco. "But the feet seemed to put the brakes on the look of the bird. The bird looked faster without its feet out. As for the junco, I wanted it making a move to get away."

The wings of both birds have the same angles. "I wanted the branch to look like a tracer of where the merlin had been."

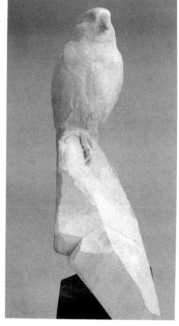

reg's first merlin, done in 1988, is a female Richardson's merlin sedately perched on a pine branch. He fanned out the tail, which is characteristic of a posed merlin.

It's difficult to tell Greg's finished carvings from the real thing. Greg owns the male Richardson's merlin pictured in these photographs. The bird shown here is one year old.

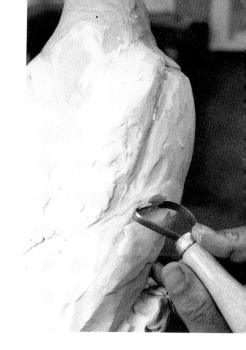

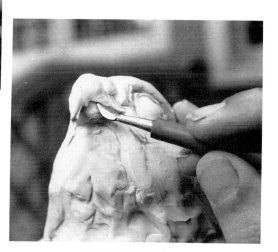

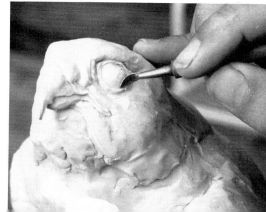

G reg was commissioned by the Ward foundation on behalf of the governor of Maryland to do a sculpture of a peregrine in clay. The sculpture was to be a gift for an official in the Middle East.

Working in Sculpey and Super Sculpey, Greg discovered he could work out problems in clay before he starts on a piece. "I can move clay around and get things flowing. I can make a fluid-looking design, because that's the nature of clay. But clay cannot be tightly detailed. The trick when working in clay is knowing when to stop."

The armature for this clay sculpture is wood, but he would rather have used a Styrofoam core to reduce the weight of the piece. When it was finished, he baked the clay for a half hour at 300 degrees and painted the hardened surface.

reg's raptors have made him money and won him some prestigious ribbons. For four years in a row his birds have taken Best-in-Show at the World Wildfowl Carving Competition. And for three years they have been featured at the Leigh Yawkey Woodson Birds in Art Exhibit.

"A Richardson's merlin, the biggest and prettiest of the merlins, is a sky-blue color."

"The Cooper's hawk
composition flows
in a strong S shape."

Greg prefers to carve in tupelo. He likes its strength, especially for making thin parts of the anatomy. "You can even go against the grain of tupelo and achieve tight details. A wood like walnut, by comparison, can be detailed well, but the grain lines will project through. This sometimes happens with tupelo, but I have an aggressive style and carve in a lot of feathers so the grain lines don't show."

"I put peregrines on rocks because their feet are adapted to rest on flat surfaces. Another raptor, such as a merlin, perches best on a branch."

Greg designed the gyrfalcon piece to have a twisted look. The falcon and the lower part of the limb were carved from a single piece of tupelo. The tucked-up foot was inserted as a separately carved piece, and the primaries are inserts.

Though the gyrfalcon is primarily white with dark barring, Greg used many different colors, especially for the breast area. For the warm areas he painted yellow to orange to green. For the cool areas he worked from blue to purple to green.

"I feel extremely fortunate that I have been able to make a living carving what I want to carve. I believe in destiny, but I believe in persistence, promotion, and talent, too. I wouldn't advise someone to quit his job and do this for a living. But for me it has worked."

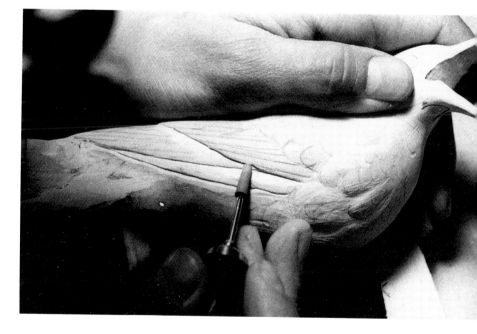

Joan and Eugene have worked with different kinds of wood but primarily their birds are sculpted from basswood and tupelo. Tupelo is very abrasive to knife steel, so when working it they must use thin-bladed knives and sharpen them frequently. The advantage of tupelo is that it textures cleanly and well. They have tried jelutong, but that wood has large pores that have to be filled before it's painted, and it has to be carved carefully to avoid splits. Basswood, tupelo, and jelutong each has its advantages, and each requires unique carving strategies. They now choose the wood that best fits a particular design and have won blue ribbons with birds carved from all three woods.

For this meadowlark they chose tupelo.

"Legs are important. A leg doesn't just hold a carving in position. It tells a lot about what the bird is doing and can imply movement. Even the placement of the toes is important. Toes tell you whether the bird is gripping or is relaxed or is holding itself against the wind. Toes tell you whether a bird wants to leave its perch or whether it's comfortable. They add an element of expressive interest and get the observer involved."

Eugene prefers copper and brass for making a bird's legs, feet, and talons. Brass has strength and ridigity and can be ground and shaped easily with needle files and carbide bits. For the toes he uses copper wire, which can be bent and rebent to position the toes.

"Welded feet are more durable and can hold a bird in position, even if it is on one leg, without sagging and bending."

The meadowlark's feet are fitted to the carved wooden rock prior to painting. A brass rod running the length of the leg into the rock holds the feet in position. The legs have been carefully positioned to hold the singing bird in just the right posture.

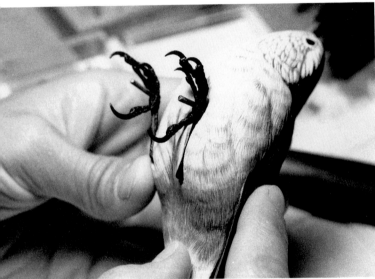

A recess was carved into the body of the bird to allow the feet and legs to push up into the soft underbelly feathers. In this composition the nuthatch is leaning forward and twisting to one side. The tarsi (lower legs) are not completely covered with feathers.

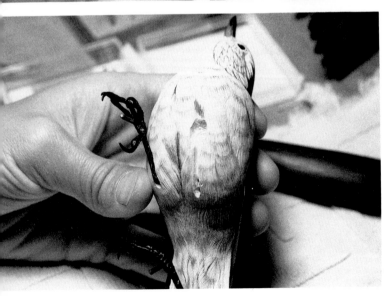

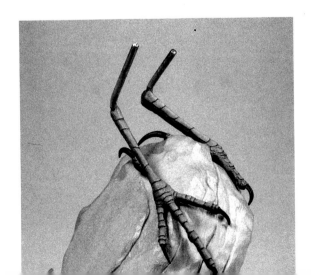

The size and shape
of the negative
space affect the
balance and impact
of the design.

Joan and Eugene use the concept of negative space in their compositions. The recognizable, represented shapes of the birds and their habitats make up the positive space, and the unoccupied area is the negative space. Negative space can echo the shape of a bird. The curve of the lower part of the branch represents the curve of the kestrel's breast. Joan reflects, "The negative space may be the most important element in the composition.

"I often find that if I feel a piece is missing something, it's because the negative space is not working. I like to study a composition, silhouetting it against a bright window to see how negative and positive space interplay. When I view a composition this way, reduced to its barest elements without the interference of color and texture, I can really critique it."

"**B**lack-capped chickadees are in demand. They're brave little birds that often interact with people, so we have a special fondness for them." Perched on the end of a branch, this chickadee is fluffed out, readjusting itself because of the cold. Despite its being at the end of a limb, it has a relaxed, comfortable feeling. The gray of the branch appropriately suggests a winter day.

F ound only in the forests and clearings of the U.S. Northwest and Western Canada, the rufous hummingbird measures three and a half to four inches long. The male is mostly rust colored with a white breast and orange-red throat.

Joan and Eugene often put their hummingbirds in flight, usually feeding from a flower. But they design perched hummingbirds as well. "Observers don't usually see these birds sitting still because they don't sit quietly for that long. The rufous hummingbird is very aggressive, constantly twisting its head, looking for another bird to chase.

"We perched the hummingbird with a rose. Its green leaves complement the green of the bird's head and suggest a warm day. We positioned the plant below the bird to break up the negative space, which could be too powerful for a small bird."

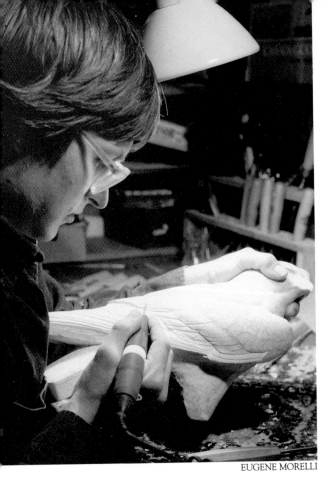

EUGENE MORELLI

EUGENE MORELLI

EUGENE MORELLI

EUGENE MORELLI

EUGENE MORELLI

In *Black Rock Tiercel*, a bold male peregrine falcon perches on top of a shard of black rock. Carved from a single piece of tupelo, the bird spreads its wings slightly, repositioning for takeoff. "I wanted the peregrine to stand out as it perched on the rock outcropping, so I decided to make the rock black and abstract, not highly detailed," says Eugene. "The rock combines the effect of a black cube, popular as a base, with the illusion of the bird's rocky habitat. The rock base consists of three separate pieces of wood held together with metal rods. We chose the color and shape of the rock with a specific effect in mind. Black seemed to be the perfect color to show off the peregrine's markings. I wanted to contrast the highly detailed bird with the stark abstractness of the rock. The rock is a much more interesting shape than just a cube would have been, and I designed it to add drama."

"We outlined the wing feathers with a grinder and then used a skew chisel to layer and shape them. We worked forward carving the feathers and details on the wings and tail and then moving to the head. We left the face and bill for last. Working in this direction makes the feathers look as if they are lying on top of each other.

"After we carve the more distinct feathers of the wings and tail, we go over all of them, refine their shapes, add more splits, ripples, and undercuts, and then take the feathers to their final thinness."

EUGENE MORELLI

LARRY STEVENS

Joan and Eugene spend time studying live birds. Eugene says, "We like to gather lots of information about our subjects before we begin a carving. We immerse ourselves in the spirit and behavior of the bird. I had seen wild peregrines on two occasions and was extremely impressed with their flying ability."

Three peregrines live nearby, and Joan and Eugene take advantage of that resource. "I am entranced by these birds," says Joan. "They have a presence and nobility about them. The face and eyes are especially beautiful, so I wanted to get that just right."

There are three subspecies of peregrine in North America. *Black Rock Tiercel* features the *Falco peregrinus anatum*, which is indigenous to most of the continental United States. It was no coincidence that two of their live models were of that subspecies. They decided to do a male bird, or tiercel, which is smaller than the female.

The live bird.

"The American tree sparrow nests far to the north and usually winters farther south than our home in Montana, so we generally see these beautiful birds during the spring and fall migrations. We timed our work on this piece to coincide with the fall migration, when the birds are in their elegant, new plumage and the chestnut-red in their heads and wings is strikingly beautiful with the fall foliage.

"A branch of wild rose, with its red hips and its red-orange leaves, sets the time of fall migration and adds additional interest to the design by balancing the visual and spatial weight of the piece. The color of the berries and leaves also adds harmony and cohesiveness to the composition."

ALL COLOR PHOTOGRAPHS COURTESY OF
EUGENE MORELLI AND JOAN ZYGMUNT

The sparrow has a characteristic central breast spot and soft, gray breast feathers. A closeup of the head and shoulders shows the chestnut crown, dark upper mandible, and white wing bars. The composition's wings feature exceptionally soft blending of colors Joan achieved using drybrush techniques with acrylic paint.

Joan and Eugene used grinding techniques for the texture of the soft feathers of the head, face, and breast, and carefully controlled burning on the more distinct feathers of the wings and tail.

Joan often uses a dry-blending technique. "This will give an amazingly soft blend where the transition is from a dark to a lighter value of the same color rather than two different colors." The gray-blue tertials of a kestrel and its fluffy, rust back feathers are painted using this method.

"We like to use poses to show a particular position that impressed us while we observed that species in the wild."

Both rely on perfectly done detailing to get soft results. "The detailing must be light and sweeping, sometimes with a split included. I use a no. 1 brush and a medium-heavy mix of the lighter value added to the edges of the painted feather. When I dip the brush into the paint, it is important not to wet the brush up the ferrule but to wet just the tip. Then I wipe the brush on my palette to take off excess paint. Using just the tip of the brush I apply color on a few barbs of the feather from a third of the barb to the tip of the barb. If done right, it will take a few passes to build up the lighter color and add more paint toward the edges."

Lazuli Bunting on Wild Rose is a beautiful western songbird that nests in abundance on Joan and Eugene's land. The birds choose the densest sites of hawthorn, chokecherry, and wild rose bushes on the otherwise dry, grassy hillsides. Wild rose is in full bloom at the start of the nesting season, and the brilliant male will sit atop the highest point of these shrubs and sing repeatedly, creating one of the most beautiful color combinations in nature.

For this piece Eugene pioneered the use of silver for the delicate flower petals and developed welding techniques to make strong, durable foliage and habitat elements. The graceful branches and flowers create a composition that is equally interesting when viewed from any direction.

Lazuli Bunting on Wild Rose took Best-in-Category for all songbirds in both the U.S. Nationals on Long Island, New York, and the 1988 World Championships in Ocean City, Maryland.

The energetic little rufous hummingbird often sits on a bare branch overlooking its feeding territory, vigorously defending it from all intruders. This simple yet elegant design portrays the male. A branch directs attention upward toward the bird, while the leaves at the base balance the composition and reintroduce the colors found on the bird's crown and back.

"We wanted to capture the feeling of a falcon hunting from a high perch. To do so, we gave the kestrel an alert and attentive posture and used negative space."

The mature male American kestrel is brilliantly colored. "Painting the American kestrel is both challenging and rewarding," says Joan. "I use numerous different blending techniques to soften the transition from one area of color to another. When painting the rust and cream colors of the back and breast, I like to express a variety of tonal qualities that enhance depth and softness and highlight the form and details."

Joan and Eugene were inspired to do this piece after they had observed a mature male whose hunting territory included the fields surrounding their home.

"With its long, slender neck and striking plumage and tail, the pintail drake is perhaps the most elegant of waterfowl. It is also a favorite of ours to carve. We're able to observe them at a nearby wildlife refuge."

"**T**he pintail's graceful shape allows for truly classical sculptured form. The subject is the entire composition." When painting the scapular feathers of a pintail, Joan will first wet a few of the feathers with plain water, allowing them to dry to a matte finish. Then she paints the dark, center color, leaving the edges unpainted. The creamy color is added to the edges of the feather adjacent to, but not touching, the center. Next, a dry fan blender is gently brushed across the lighter color against the grain of the burning lines until it barely touches the darker color. Detail that is either ground or burnt in too deeply will produce choppy blending.

"The white-to-black transition on the tertial and scapular feathers and the vermiculation on the sides are some of the most challenging elements to paint."

"We wanted to portray a feeling of energy and movement essential to hummingbirds."

The male calliope, with its bright gorget flashing in the sun, hovers and prepares to feed. The female stretches and watches intently. The honeysuckle vine, welded of brass, copper, and silver, surrounds and focuses attention on these tiny, energetic birds. "These birds are so full of life and so captivating to watch."

The piece was awarded Best-in-Category for songbirds and Best-in-Show for life-sized waterfowl at the U.S. Nationals in 1991.

In *Black Rock Tiercel*, the alert and powerful peregrine prepares for flight by stepping and beginning to open its wings. Joan and Eugene captured the bold presence of the falcon perched atop a shard of rock. "We wanted the entire composition to reflect the confidence that emanates from these magnificent birds."

The piece took seconds in birds of prey and overall at the 1990 Long Island Wildfowl Carving Competition in Port Washington, New York, as well as Best-in-Category for birds of prey and second overall at the 1991 U.S. Nationals.

The sharp-edged, abstract rock adds to the drama of the sculpture, the blackness contrasting and intensifying the colors of this regal bird.

Joan and Eugene put a great deal of expression into their work. "Wildfowl art is like playing a musical instrument. You need to know the notes and put feeling into them."